How
To Be
An...

IMPACT
MAN

In your family, work, church and beyond

Dr. Paul J. Young

How to be an...

IMPAC†MAN

CHANGING OUR...
- *Selves*
- *Homes*
- *Places of Work*
- *Churches*
- *World*

Dr. Paul J. Young

Now is the time

Today is the day

To begin

And keep on beginning

Every single day

To keep going

To make MY MARK

FOR Christ and

WITH Christ

For my family

For His Church

For my community

Forever

Amen

Read This First

No one discards a box of delicious fried chicken because it has bones. No! You grab a piece, eat the meat and discard the bones.

So to with this book. Eat the meat - there is a lot here to chew on, to think about, process and pray about. If you find any bones, discard them. Why waste all the meat because there are a few bones! (No book authored by a human is perfect, you know).

Most of all, why not use this IMPACT MAN book to change your life and the lives of others?

Read. Drink in the principles.

Pray. Blast through the solitary life, isolated that is crippling so many men today.

Reap a great harvest with a life or many lives changed through your powerful, Holy Spirit guided prayers and actions.

Bravo!

Forward

Rev. Frank Epperson, Rector
Saint Eugene's Cathedral
Santa Rosa, California

Dr. Paul Young is a dynamic, valued member of my parish. As a Protestant minister, he accomplished amazing things due to his love of God and his boundless energy. Now, as a Catholic, he takes this love one step further by calling men to affirm and strengthen their Catholic faith and thus, transform themselves, their families and their community by being men of IMPACT.

In the culture and time that we live in, men are often confused about what it means to be Godly. They want to be held to a higher standard, to establish a prayer life, to live holy lives - they just don't know how to begin. By being part of a group of men who have the same goals and aspirations, Catholic men can transform themselves into holy men and, ultimately, they can change the world, one person at a time.

Dr. Young points out the power that is to be found in prayer (especially the Rosary), reading the Holy Bible, in making good and frequent sacramental Confession and in receiving Christ in Holy Communion. This power, which is the Holy Spirit working in us, is what transforms us.

As Rector of a large parish, I definitely see the need for men to step up to the plate and reclaim their position as leaders of their families and communities. With the help of committed Catholics like Dr. Paul Young and his book, *How To Be An IMPACT MAN,* I see how this can become a reality.

A DRPAULPRESS.COM **publication**

Dedicated to **Tateos Nigohosyan**, a native of Bulgaria, whom I helped to begin on the pathway of faith when I headed up the Jesus Film Team ministry in Bulgaria. He is now impacting thousands in Bulgaria and beyond.

I thank God for you, Tateos, everyday in my prayer, thanking God for your faith, work and love for the Kingdom of God. May your breed increase!

This book is also dedicated to a group of men who have helped me initiate the IMPACT MAN movement, **Greg Harder, Greg De-Gennaro, Bill Peter, Michael Diepenbrock, Brad Nicholls, Patrick Welter,** and **Chris Young**. You guys are such dear friends in the faith. Thanks for your willingness to develop the IMPACT MAN movement. Heaven will be welcoming many more men into its fold because of you.

To **Saint Joseph,** our Patron Saint

Pray for us that we might be IMPACT men
Men who are brave and courageous
Men intent on one thing
    To be change agents in our
            Families
            Places of work
            Churches
            Communities
            World
    Reaching other men
            To be IMPACT MEN
            For the glory of Christ.
                Amen

Table of Contents

Appendix D

How To Study The Bible In The Original Languages (Hebrew, Greek) as an aid for Lectio Divina

Appendix E

Men's groups and resources

How To Be An I.M.P.A.C.T. Man

Intimacy with Jesus

Mission - living life on purpose

Power that comes from purity

Anchored in the Faith

Committed to other men

Triumphant!

INTRODUCTION

THE TIME IS NOW!

There has been so much talk over that last few decades about evangelization - growing the Church. Yet the Catholic Church will be half the size it is today if something is not done. More and more people are being born, but not enough are being *born again* - baptized and committed to their Catholic faith, IMPACTing their world for Christ.

IF NOT NOW...WHEN?
IF NOT I...WHO?

If you were the CEO of a large corporation and the numbers were sliding like they are in the Catholic Church, you would be worried. What can we do to turn the tide?

Do we sit around and wring our hands? No!

There is something you can do as a man. You can become an IMPACT man and see revolutionary changes happen, in your life, your family, your place of work, your Church and your world.

As you read this book, you will be given a plan with specifics, a game plan to change the world where you live. This plan is going to alter the kind of man that you are, in your family, your workplace, your Church and the community where you live.

In the next few years you are going to see things happen that are beyond your dreams. Men are going to be IMPACTED, homes changed, Churches will be renewed, and the society where you live will be utterly changed. It's going to be revolutionary. In fact, IT WILL BE A REVOLUTION, as men, beginning with you, begin to BE MEN, to man up - to be the kind of real men God uses.

It's been around 2,000 years since the early disciples began to gather around Jesus to form a band of men who would ultimately change the world. Jesus wants YOU to continue the process.

As you read this book, pay attention to the word, IMPACT. As you do, begin putting into practice each letter of the word, I.M.P.A.C.T. and you will never be the same!

Intimacy with Jesus.
Mission with family, work, Church, world
Power that comes from purity.
Anchored in the faith.
Committed to other men.
Triumphant - on the winning side.

I WAS MADE FOR THIS HOUR

GOD PLANNED THAT I BE HERE TO CHANGE
- *MY FAMILY*
- *MY PLACE OF WORK*
- *MY CHURCH*
- *MY NEIGHBORHOOD*
- *MY WORLD*

TO IMPACT THEM WITH THE GOOD NEWS
- *WITH JOY*
- *WITH HOPE*
- *WITH PASSION*
- *WITH LOVE*

TO BE A MAN FOR THE KINGDOM OF GOD AND HIS CHURCH

TO MAKE AN IMPACT
- *NOW*
- *TODAY*
- *TOMORROW*
- *THE REST OF MY LIFE*

FOR THE GLORY OF GOD
> *AMEN*

PART 1

INTIMACY WTIH JESUS

A LOVE FOR...*GOD*

CHAPTER 1

THE NEED

How many men live the Christian life without Christ? Oh yes, they have the Church - all the activities, going to Church, being involved in the organization, the people, making friends, all the social stuff that goes on. But Jesus? We know who he is, but DO WE KNOW HIM?

It was John, the disciple of Christ, who wrote in his Gospel:

> *This is eternal life that they might KNOW...Jesus Christ.*
>
> John 17:2

Solomon had just become King of Israel, following his father David, one of the greatest Kings who has ever lived. David, Solomon's father, was called a "friend of God," so close was their relationship. We see that friendship unfold in many of the Psalms King David wrote.

Solomon was a young man who desired to be like his father, to lead his people faithfully.

One night, in a dream, God came to Solomon and said: "Ask anything you want, and I will give it to you."
Imagine. Anything you want!

Most of us would ask for our bank accounts or stock portfolios to be filled with millions of dollars, or to have a new home or other material stuff. Others may ask for a new wife, or for better relationships, for honor, for the recognition we feel we deserve, and on and on.

What would this young king ask for?

Notice his request, a deep desire that was life changing.

> *Give me a hearing heart.*
> I Kings 3:9

In other words, Solomon asked for a "heart with ears on it." He wanted to be able to hear God's voice deep in the recesses of his soul, where God loves to commune with us.

Brian came to me with a depression and void that he couldn't seem to fill. His wife died of cancer after being married for 52 years. It was over a year now, and the pain of this loss should have begun to heal. But not for Brian. Though he was deeply involved in his Church, it was the times around the home that got to him. The absence of his wife was like a constant dripping faucet. And he sat around the house, moping.

"I don't know what to do," Brian said tearfully. "She was my dearest friend, my soulmate, my life."

As I got to know Brian, I recognized a man who was very committed to his faith. He had been a Christian most of his life and had served God faithfully. Yet there was this hole, this void in his life that gnawed at his soul, a gnawing that wouldn't quit.

Over the decades I have had helping people, I find that as we age, God allows circumstances, events that come into our lives, to prepare us for heaven. He begins to remove those things that have gotten in the way of a deeper relationship with him, the job, raising children, dependance on others, various activities like golf, football, baseball, or other outdoor or social activities. And then there we are...sitting at home with time on our hands.

And that's what God wants...time on our hands.

For he is sitting there with us, wanting a deeper relationship.

Yet too often we ignore him, the source of life and joy. We turn on the TV, read a book, surf the web, or go to a ball game to deaden the pain of our boredom and loneliness. Day after day that occurs when all the while Jesus is knocking at our soul's door, asking to come in, to be at home in our lives and for us to be at home with him.

What was happening with Brian, happens to so many who not only lose a mate through death, but men who are too busy for a personal relationship with God. They are involved with the Church, but not in a personal, INTIMATE relationship with Jesus.

I turned to Brian and said. " Brian, you are not alone in that house. Someone is there with you who wants to get acquainted with you on a much deeper level."

"What are you talking about," he questioned?

"God."

Brian looked puzzled as he spoke. "But I go to Church, help lead our men's fellowship group, and am on the church board. What more does God want?"

"YOU," I said softly, trying not to shock him.

"Me," Brian retorted?

What was happing here is what happens with so many men. They get tied up with Church, with their religious activities, with the social events of the Church...

Going, going, going...

Doing, doing, doing...

And miss out on the PERSON who wants to get to know them, the founder of the Church, Jesus Christ our Lord.

The Church was never meant to fill the soul. All the activities and great causes, no matter how good, are not meant in the end to satisfy the human heart. Too many get caught up in "*churchianity*" and miss out on Christianity. They miss out on Christ, like Martha did in the accounts of Mary and Martha in the Scriptures.

Some of you know that I became a Catholic after being a Protestant Evangelical pastor for 35 years and helped grow one of the largest churches in the Dallas Fort Worth area. Why would I do that? It seemed that I had everything a pastor would want. I did, in one sense. But I knew there was more.

I wanted more of JESUS…in a way I couldn't get him in a Protestant church.

You see, the central focus of the Catholic Mass is Jesus. The first half of the Mass is focused on Scriptures that lead us to JESUS (one reading from the Old Testament, then we sing one of the Psalms, another reading comes from the Epistles or other New Testament book and then climaxing with a reading from the Gospels where Jesus speaks to us).

After that there is a Homily (a short sermon) on the Scriptures that were read. In all, around 35 percent of the Mass is pure Scripture. St. Paul states to Timothy: "Do not neglect the reading of Scripture."

So the first half of the Mass is Scripture focused, the WORD of the Lord.

The second half of the Mass is focused purely on JESUS, the WORD made incarnate, the Word who came to give his life as a ransom for many. It is here that a miracle happens at every Mass. Bread and wine become the actual body and blood of Christ Jesus our Lord. We see it happen with our physical and spiritual eyes.

Jesus comes in a very special way - fully, with his body, blood, soul and divinity.

"The whole substance of the bread is changed into the whole substance of Christ's body, and the whole substance of the wine into the whole substance of Christ's blood. The 'accidents' - color, texture, shape, and so on - remain those of bread and wine. But the substance, the very nature of this reality, is now Christ's body and blood" (Thomas Aquinas).

While this happens we are all on our knees in reverence and adoration. Jesus is here unlike at any other time. It is an awesome occasion, a holy time, as we contemplate HIS presence. St. Paul says in Corinthians 11, that angels flock to see this event happen because it is so hallowed and divine.

The Mass ends by people lining up to RECEIVE JESUS, actually, physically, totally into their lives.

The deep magic (words C. S. Lewis loves to use in his books about Narnia) of this event is beyond comprehension. It is what history is all about, Jesus restoring the human race to its place of dignity and divinity. We all receive the LIFE OF CHRIST as our food that changes us, bringing us back to what we should have been.

Yet, even in this place, in the Catholic Church, millions of people take this spiritual manna and act without understanding. They go through the motions, these sacred actions without being moved in their hearts and souls. And though Jesus is actually present in them, they ignore him, the fountain of life.

It is a tragedy beyond understanding!

No wonder there is so much depression, despair, anxiety and purposeless living. They are blind, men living on the animal plane and not rising to and living in that spiritual dimension in the presence of Christ, the one who continues to prove his love for us. To ignore him, to put him on the back shelf is to doom our lives.

So no matter how often you go to Church, you can still miss Jesus. He gets shoved to the side of your life.

No wonder so many men have an emptiness in their souls that gnaws at them. Your soul cries for HIM, but you stuff it with the busyness of Church, with activities, with sports, with food, with TV, with so many other substitutes.

In the book of Revelation, chapter 3, Jesus is seen as speaking to a Church, wanting to be part of their lives. All that churchiness, and too often not much Jesus.

So Jesus says:

> *Look! I am standing at your souls door and knocking. I will not break down the door and come in. You must open the door and let me in. If you do, we will converse and eat together as friends. We will laugh, cry, and have a conversation that will warm both of our hearts. I am looking for a confidant, someone to talk with. And you need me, for I am the source of life and joy. Open that rusty hinged door. If you do, I promise to come in and fill all your heart's desire.*
>
> Revelation 3:20 expanded

How long had Jesus been knocking at Brian's door?

I have found that years and years go by and the tender, determined Jesus keeps knocking. We hear the knocks and, as if there is a solicitor at the door, we ignore him thinking that he will go. After all, we are so busy. There is the book to read, the TV show to watch, the kids activities to go to, a game to attend, and all the Church and social obligations.

But he persists. Knocking. Knocking. Knocking.

I continued my conversation with Brian.

"I want you to buy a paper back Bible, one you can write in and underline the special things God will be saying to you. You see, if you are going to allow Jesus to be part of your life, if you want him to be your shepherd, you need to daily read and meditate on the Scriptures. It was St. Jerome who said:"

Ignorance of Scriptures is ignorance of Christ.

"So, Brian, you are going to begin a journey into the heart of Jesus and let him speak to you in ways you never thought possible."

"I also want you to go to the stationary store and buy a tablet or a diary. This is going to become one of your most prized possessions after a few weeks and months. In this diary you are going to start recording your conversations with God."
Brian sat there looking confused.

"But I don't have conversations with God," he said. "I pray, you know, the usual prayers for my kids, our Church, my health. But that's about it."

"Brian, I'm going to teach you how to listen to God," I spoke, seeking to encourage him. And then I shared with him the story about King Solomon and his desire to hear God.

"You've got ears. You just need to learn how to use them. Because when you do, you will never have that aching loneliness in your heart again. Of course you will always miss your wife. But God is using this loneliness you feel to draw you closer to him. He is at the door of your heart and wants to put a balm on your aching soul, and bring joy and purpose back into your life."

Brian turned and spoke with hope in his voice. "I want that more than anything. I want to learn how to use the ears on my heart."

What Brian needed to learn was how to abide in Christ as taught by Jesus in the Gospel of John chapter 15. He needed to learn how to drink in the sap from the vine, the presence and person of Jesus, dining with him, sharing things in common, being confidants of each other at a depth that would fill the heart with a satisfaction and joy that is uncommon with most Christians, even those who serve faithfully.

Yet this is what we were made for. Adam and Eve had it before sin entered the human race, and since then we have shut God out, leaving him knocking at the door.

All the while there is that ache without him. The soul is thirsty, hungry for God.

> *As the deer longs for streams of water, my soul longs for you O God. My being thirsts for God, the living God.*
>
> Psalm 42:1

An old song in response to that image of Christ knocking at the door of our lives puts it this way:

> *Into my heart*
> *Into my heart*
> *Come into my heart*
> *Lord Jesus*
> *Come in today*
> *Come in to stay*
> *Come into my heart*
> *Lord Jesus*

Brian needed to let Jesus in.

So many today accept Christ as their personal Lord and Savior. They acknowledge their sin, accept Christ's payment for them on the cross and receive that redemptive provision that Jesus made for them. They are then baptized, placed into Christ and Christ into them. But this is just the beginning. Jesus is their savior but hasn't become their personal friend, their confidant, sharing the deepest things together in an openness and honesty that only comes from this kind of friendship.

Brian was going to learn how to go on a treasure hunt into the heart of God - opening his ears to the voice of deity, fellowshipping with God in a way he had never done before. And once he learned how to make that journey into the heart of God, his aching soul would be healed. Brian would never be lonely or suffer from debilitating depression again.

This is the secret to the Christian life, the secret to joy, all found in the Solomon principle - having ears on our hearts, listening to the voice of our Savior, sharing together in this holy friendship and receiving the fruit of it - JOY THAT IS COMPLETE.

That's what Brian wanted, and so do you, don't you?

Well, Brian came back to the next session with his Bible and diary and said:

"Now what do I do to listen to God, to go deeper in my relationship?"

What I told him is in the next chapter. Buckle your seat belt. This is going to put you into another realm in your spiritual life, a sacred place where you may have never entered before. And the result…you will become an IMPACT man!

CHAPTER 2

BECOMING CHRIST'S CONFIDANT

Brian came into my office with a new paperback Bible and a nice journal he had picked up at his local book store. He had a smile on his face, telling me that he was ready to get deeper with God. I greeted him, complemented him on the Bible and journal he bought, and then said:

"I'm going to teach you how to listen to God. In fact, the sign of being a true Christian is that we can hear God's voice."

"Brian," I said, "Take your Bible and turn to John 10. I want you to read verse twenty-seven."

Brian fumbled with his Bible, trying to find the Gospel of John. I could tell he was not very familiar with were to look. I helped him find the place and he began to read:

> ***My sheep hear my voice.*** *I know them, and they follow me. I give them eternal life, and they shall never perish.*

"Now read verse 2-4," I said.

*The gatekeeper opens it for him, and **the sheep hear his voice**, as he calls his own sheep by name and leads them out. When he has driven out all his own, he walks ahead of them and the sheep follow him, because **they recognize his voice**.*

"Wow, I've never read this before," Brian exclaimed. "I don't believe that I would recognize Jesus' voice. That frightens me."

"It should," I responded.

"The Christian life is a personal relationship with Jesus, not just a belief system that we practice at Church. After all, 'Faith comes by hearing...' (Romans 10:17) and not just through reading the Scripture."

Then I said something to Brian that would encourage him and take away some of his fear.

"You probably know Jesus better than you give yourself credit for. Within a few weeks you are going to be better at recognizing his voice."

Then I told him a story about an experience I had while working in Sofia, Bulgaria.

I was coming down with friends from Mt. Vitosha when I noticed a disturbing thing. Up ahead were two flocks of sheep, lead by shepherds, and they were on a collision course. Within a minute or so the flocks would merge and, I thought, it would be a big mess.

We all watched as this apparent catastrophe was about to happen. Sure enough the flocks merged and became one.

But, to our surprise, something absolutely remarkable occurred. The flocks that merged were all of a sudden two flocks again with each shepherd calling out to his sheep to follow him. They KNEW his voice, and they followed him.

Within a few minutes we were sitting in a cafe having coffee and talking about what we had seen. It brought back John 10, and how Jesus leads us, as it says in John 10:10, to a life that is abundant.

Hearing Jesus' voice is so important. In John 15, the abiding chapter, Jesus says in verse 7:

If you abide in me and my WORDS abide in you, ask for whatever you desire and it will be done to you.

There are two basic words for *word* in the greek Bible, the original language the New Testament was written in. One is logos. Jesus is called the eternal logos in John 1:1. This refers to all that is revealed - the totally. We are called to believe in this totality, the logos when we become Christians.

But there is another word for *word* that fits in to what I was talking about with Brian. It is the word, *rhema,* a greek word referring to a word that is fresh, spoken at that moment, hot. It's the difference between reading a letter I sent you or listening to me in person. They are both good, but one is fresh, relational, something you can interact with in time and space.

I wanted Brian to experience *rhema,* the words of Jesus spoken to him, to his sheep, personally, fresh words that would guide his life and give him encouragement. I wanted him to take the logos (the written Bible) and allow it to become *rhema* - hot, fresh, the words of God spoken at the moment when he was reading the logos (the written message).

Brian seemed to be drinking in what I was talking about - being a sheep, listening to the voice, the words (rhema) of Jesus.

"How do I do that," Brian inquired? "I want to hear the voice of Jesus, like those sheep heard the voice of the shepherd you talked about."

"Now, Brian, you are going to see that what the prophet Isaiah said is true when he said:"

My thoughts are not your thoughts nor my ways your ways.

"You are going to discover the thoughts of God and his ways or actions."

It is in this step, if we are listening to Jesus, that he is going to give us **HIS** interpretation of every event that happens to us and **HIS** action steps to take in response to those events. It is here that HIS THOUGHTS and HIS WAYS become our thoughts and ways."

His ways were revealed to Moses, his mighty deeds to the people of Israel

Psalm 103:7

"Moses had a much deeper relationship with God than the average Israelite. They were focused on a God who could do something for them. Their thoughts were selfish thoughts - "give me," thoughts. Moses, however, had become a confidant of God and could interact with him as a friend to a friend. He knew how God worked and even, at times, counseled God!"

"It was King David, a man after the heart of God, a man who knew God's voice in a most intimate way, who wrote in Psalm 25:"

> *Make known to me your ways, LORD*
> *Teach me your paths*
> *Guide me in your truth*
> *Teach me*
> *For you are God, my savior*

"You see, Brian, to know the shepherd we need to know his thoughts and ways. And…

WE CAN!"

St. Paul said to the Church at Corinth (I Corinthians 2: 10-12),

> *These things God has revealed to us through the Spirit; for the Spirit searches everything, even the DEPTHS OF GOD. For what human being knows what is truly human except the human spirit that is within? So also no one comprehends what is truly God's except the Spirit of God. Now we have received not the spirit of the world, but the Spirit that is from God, SO*

THAT WE MAY UNDERSTAND *the gifts bestowed on us by* *God.*

"Brian, this is what your heart longs for, these deep things of God. And it is available to you because through your baptism, you received the Holy Spirit who will guide you into all truth."

"I want to show you the process of hearing *rhema,* words of Jesus that he will speak to you in the moment, guiding you, words that will encourage you, move you, give you insight in what to do."

Brian sat there listening to what I was saying, drinking it all in. Then he spoke:

"I want to do that more than anything."

"First," I said, "set aside a place in your home where you are going to meet God, a place that is conducive for prayer and meditation. Some people will light a candle. Others put on quiet, meditative music, others sit in silence.

If you only did this 15 minutes a day you would spend over 90 hours with God a year!

If you spent time with God this way 5 days a week you would spend 65 hours with God. This all has a cumulative effect as you get to know God better each day. Spending 15 minutes with someone is not much. But when you spend 65 or over 90 hours with someone, you get to know them very well. And, if you do that for a number of years - you and God will become very good friends, and he will share very intimate things with you."

"But you have to begin," I said, emphasizing the importance of what I wanted Brian to do.

As you read this, I want you to see the great value of spending time with God - abiding in him. It is THE THING that will help you to become an IMPACT man with an abiding JOY that will be unspeakable.

I turned to Brian and said: " We are going to start with a very familiar Bible passage, Psalm 23. Turn to it in your Bible."

Brian found the Psalms and turned to the 23rd chapter.

"Before reading any passage, Brian, it is always good to make sure that the pathway into your heart is clean. If the pipeline is dirty or plugged, you won't be hearing much from God. The intimacy will be broken."

John said in I John 1:

If we walk in the light as Jesus is in the light we will have fellowship with each other and the blood of Jesus will cleanse us from all sin...if we confess our sin he is faithful and just to forgive us our sin and to cleanse us from all unrighteousness.

"Brian, a number of Christians never hear from God because of sin in their life. Often this sin is simply the sin of not abiding in

Christ, walking with him, fellowshipping on a daily basis, moment by moment. In fact, it is simply the sin of ignoring God - doing our own thing without being conscious of his presence."

"I find a good prayer to prepare me for this is the one King David prayed at the end of Psalm 139:"

> *Search me oh God and know my heart*
> *Test me and know my thoughts*
> *Point out anything in me that offends you*
> *And lead me into your everlasting ways*

"After I examine my conscience waiting for the Holy Spirit to point out my sin and acknowledge that sin to God, I then spend just a moment in thanksgiving for God's grace and goodness. When we come to God with praise on our tongue, he loves that, and he loves to open himself up to us, to confide in us on the deepest level.

As Catholics, the sacrament of confession is a beautiful thing where you will confess your sins to God through a Priest and find total cleansing. The kind of confession I am talking about, however, is daily confession, making sure you are clean before proceeding with an open heart before God.

After examination of my conscience and acknowledging my sin and then thanking God for his grace and forgiveness, I always pray a simple prayer of preparation before I begin to read the Bible. It's a prayer found in Psalm 119:18:"

Open my eyes LORD, that I may clearly see what you have in your word.

"St. Paul prayed a similar prayer that you could pray found in Ephesians chapter 1, when he says:"

I pray that the eyes of my heart may be enlightened to see all that God has for me.
Ephesians 1:18, paraphrased and personalized

"Brian, God is more interested in this relationship with you than you could ever imagine. You don't have to beg him to show up as you spend time in the Scripture. He will be there, waiting for you to be open to him. In the next few weeks you are going to learn better and better how to listen to him and recognize his voice."

Then I looked at Brian and said: "Now I want to give you an assignment to do before our next session. I want you to spend at least 5 days learning to listen to God using Psalm 23. Here's what I want you to do on each day."

DAY 1: Read in a prayerful way Psalm 23 in its entirety. Write down one word that describes what this psalm is talking about. What is the basic thrust of this psalm? This word will help you focus on that. Be sure and use your journal as you write this down. After you come up with this one word, ask God how this word applies to your life today. Write this down.
When you ask God questions, you can almost be certain that when an answer suddenly comes into your mind, it's God talking with you (you are hearing his voice like the sheep hear the shepherd's

voice). Don't question it (unless it's not in line with the Christian faith). God wants to speak to you. He is interested in every facet of your life. Let him do it.

After you have heard from God, thank him. Spend time praising and adoring him. This pleases him and will bless you.

DAY 2: Read Psalm 23 again, prayerfully, and underline the key words or phrases that speak to you. Jesus is going to highlight some words or phrases for you and will talk to you about them. Write them in your journal. For example, you might underline every time it says, "my" in the passage, or all the active verbs like, "he leads," he guides," "he restores," as well as other words or phrases. Look at these key words or phrases and let God speak to you about each one. What is he saying to you about those words. Write it down.

Ask God to be specific. He wants to guide you, to be YOUR shepherd. And he is doing it NOW! Be sure and thank him for what he is showing you.

DAY 3: Today I want you to think through your life and how God has shepherded you. Prayerfully read the psalm and note the ways Jesus made sure that you lacked nothing that you really needed. Write down:
1. How he made you lie down
2. Restored your soul
3. Guided you
4. Was at your side when you went through the dark valleys
5. How he has provided many good things for you (list them)

6. How he is planning to provide a future joy of spending an eternity with him now and in heaven...forever.

This should be a history of Jesus' movement in your life up to the present.

Think through the segments - childhood, young adult, middle age, retirement. Walk with God through these times, let him show you how he was with you. Write them down. As you do so, praise him for being your shepherd.

DAY 4: Read Psalm 23 again, but this time I want you to go to your Catholic Church. Take your Bible and journal and read it slowly in front of the crucifix. As you enter the Church you will notice a red candle burning up front, by the Tabernacle that houses the actual presence of Jesus in the form of bread that has been consecrated. Jesus is totally there, physically, emotionally, and spiritually.

Jesus wants to talk with you from the cross and from his Tabernacle and will give you new insight to Psalm 23. Be still. Worship. Listen. Write down what Jesus is saying to you. Remember his words will come as impressions to your mind, thoughts that will show up that are not ordinarily there.

Brian, as you see Jesus on the cross, your shepherd, know that Jesus wants you on the cross with him, to give yourself away for others even as he did. He is calling you to be a shepherd to others just like he is to you and all those who follow him. Who in your family does he want you to shepherd? Who does he want you to love in your neighborhood, your Church? Write this down. Jesus wants you to receive his love, but to also give it. He does not want you to be just a taker but also a giver - helping to take care of the needs of others.

This is a holy time, Brian. We have talked about ABIDING in Christ. The great fruit of this is LOVE of others.

DAY 5: Get in your big easy chair. Move it back so you are in a comfortable, relaxed state. As you recline, allow Psalm 23 to become more real to you as you picture yourself resting in the arms of Jesus your shepherd.

Moses said:
> *The eternal God is our refuge and his everlasting arms are under you, supporting you.*
>
> Deuteronomy 33:27

Let God embrace you as your loving shepherd. Breathe in slowly as you remember that the breath God gave Adam and Eve, in the beginning of time, is in you. Let that breath move in and out restfully, deeply, breathing in God's life, breathing out anything that is not of God. This helps you to relax and receive his embrace. Don't say anything. Just be in his loving presence.

At times you can let your mind flow to Psalm 23 and the restoration God wants to bring to your soul. Receive it. Let your soul drink in the presence of the loving, caring God. This time in the chair is a time for contemplation where you don't have to say anything nor does God have to say a word. You are being together, to be one with each other, to enjoy each others presence.

After a period of 10 or so minutes, write down your impressions and what God may have been doing with you.

At the end of these five days you will have begun a journey into the heart of God.

Brian not only agreed to do the assignments, but smiled as I handed him the outline for the 5 days. We prayed and then he left with a new spring in his step. He was going to experience how God wanted him to be his confidant, to live in continual fellowship with the Father, Son and Holy Spirit.

Why don't you do the same assignments. It could make the difference that you are looking for.

CHAPTER 3

ABIDING LESSONS

If you will whatever God wills, you will always have exactly what you want. When you want anything else, you are not happy before you get it, and when you do get it, you do not want it. That is why you are 'up' today and 'down' tomorrow. You will never be happy if your happiness depends on getting solely what you want. Change the focus. Get a new center. Will what God wills, and your joy no man shall take from you.

Archbishop Fulton J. Sheen

As Brian came into my office he was bubbling over with excitement and joy. What a difference a week makes! I smiled as he aggressively shook my hand.

"Tell me how your week went with God."

Brian opened up his journal and began to share.

"The first day I felt a little uneasy. I have never done anything like this before. I struggled with doubts like, 'What if this doesn't work for me?' but overcame them as soon as I dug into Psalm 23."
"The key word I wrote down was shepherd. This psalm is talking about all the things the LORD our shepherd does for us.

Dr. Paul, I looked up what a shepherd did in Palestine and it's exactly what the shepherd of this psalm does. The shepherd is always with his sheep, guarding them, guiding them, making sure they have food and water. As I reflected on Jesus, my shepherd, I asked him if he wanted to say anything to me. All of a sudden, like you said, there were words in my mind that captured my thoughts. I wrote down what Jesus was saying."

I love you Brian. I have always been with you as a shepherd, guiding you, guarding you even in the hard times like you have gone through losing your wife. I was there with you when she breathed her last, and you felt so empty. I have always been there waiting for you to come to me and find rest in your soul. You are mine, Brian, and I will never leave you.

Brian wiped away tears from his eyes as he finished. I could tell that this message from Jesus had deeply moved him.

"Wow. That's great, Brian," I replied. "You were carrying on a conversation with God."

"Yes, Dr. Paul, I was," Brian said with joy written all over his face. "This was a real breakthrough for me."

"What happened on day two," I inquired.

"I did as you said, I underlined key words in the passage, words that spoke to me."

"The first word I underlined was 'nothing', where the psalmist said that with the LORD our shepherd, we lack NOTHING. When I underlined that word I was stopped in my tracks. Nothing meant exactly what it said, nothing. But was that true, I thought? Don't I lack things, particularly a wife that I loved for decades? And my body is beginning to fall apart. I have bad knees, my heart is not working like it should, and I don't sleep the way I used to. Then my three children, they don't seem to care that much about me, are too busy to drop by and chat. There were other things that came to mind about that word 'nothing'."

"How did you resolve this," I asked?

"I wrote out a question for the LORD. 'What do you mean that if you are my shepherd I will lack nothing?' Then I waited for just a few seconds when a thought came out of nowhere. God spoke, at least I think he spoke, and said:"

You will lack nothing because I am with you. I am everything. When you have me you will have all that you will ever need and more. Your wife is gone, and because she was a faithful Catholic, deeply devoted to me, you should not worry about her future as well as your future with her. She has trusted in my grace, and you should too! You have bad knees and heart, and you don't sleep so well. But I am there to give you strength to

49

carry on. And one day I will give you new knees, a new heart, and you will be able to rest like a baby. Your children may not treat you like you desire, but if you follow me fully, if you trust that my presence is always with you, I will take care of your children and make things right. Trust me. I am all you need. Without me you have nothing. But with me you have EVERY-THING, and thus YOU LACK NOTHING!

"Dr. Paul, that was so encouraging, the words of Jesus. My life is radically changing as I learn how to carry on a conversation with God, learning to ABIDE in Jesus. You are right, when I spend time with the PERSON, he gives me the PRODUCT that I desire - JOY!"

"Fantastic, Brian. You have come so far in just a few days of meditation on Psalm 23. What else did you underline on day 2?"

Brian shared with me other words he underlined that meant a lot to him, words like lead, restore, guide, dark valley, my, overflows, dwell, forever. He interacted with Jesus on each of these words and found his living LORD was there to interact with him, dialoging with him, being his PERSONAL Savior, Shepherd, and Confidant.

When Brian shared with me day 3, it showed that he was continuing to make breakthroughs as he spent time, praying this passage, interacting with Jesus, talking to him, listening, asking questions, waiting for the answers. Brian commented on the six questions I had him cover and how the LORD led him as his shepherd.

1. How *he made you lie down* - Brian focused on the word, "made" and said that God grabbed his attention, especially after his wife died. This *forced* him to rethink his life as he became depressed and alone.

2. *Restored your soul* - Brian was beginning to find the restoration he longed for as he began to drink from an on-going relationship with God.

3. *Guided you* - Brian thought through his entire life, looking at all the situations that happened to him, his parents, school, work, family, problems - all of it. He had never looked at the way God had guided him, protected him, been with him through all of his life experiences. Brian thought of one time, as a teenager, driving on an icy road. The car began to slip toward a ravine with a raging river below. He knew that this could very well mean death. But then, all of a sudden his car stopped sliding. What happened? He drove home shaking, but happy that he was still alive. On reflecting on that incident, Brian realized that his shepherd was there guiding, protecting, saving him. Then he paused to thank the LORD for his love and constant presence.

4. Was at your side when you *went through the dark valleys* - Brian still felt raw feelings from the death of his wife. At the time he didn't feel Jesus' presence. But now he knew he was there all the time, to support, comfort, be there to pray to and find strength to make it through that time of grief.

5. How he has *provided* many good things for you (list them) - Brian listed many material things, home, savings, as well as friends and family. As he began to write out his list, Brian said that he even thought of the gift of electricity, or the glasses he wore so he could see better. That opened the door to literally hundreds of things he listed. He drew up a gratitude list - one he wanted to use on a regular basis.

6. How he is planning to provide a *future joy* of spending an eternity with him now and in heaven...forever. Brian smiled as he thought about his shepherd, Jesus Christ, providing for him and his family a future full of hope. As I looked at Brian I could see that his depression was gone as he learned more and more how to listen to and abide in Christ Jesus, his shepherd.

After spending time on this assignment, Brian thanked God for being with him in so many junctures of his life. He asked Jesus to forgive him for not being aware of his continual presence as his personal, loving shepherd. "I didn't know you were there," he said. Then he thought of the picture of the person who asked God where was he when he was going through all his struggles. "I see only one set of foot prints," the man said. Then Jesus answered. "You are right, there is only one set of foot prints, mine as I carried you!"

As Brian reflected on this, he could sense Jesus saying the same thing to him, particularly as he faced the death of his wife and the loneliness that followed. Brian wrote in his journal what Jesus said:

I was with you all the time, caring for you, trying to get your attention so that you could trust me more.

"I didn't know," Brian said, shaking his head.

We both sat there for a moment, thanking God for his continual presence and not giving up on us.

Then Brian moved on to Day 4, going to his Catholic Church and praying Psalm 23 before the crucifix.

I had told him that: "Jesus wants to talk with you from the cross and from his Tabernacle and will give you new insight to Psalm 23. Be still. Worship. Listen. Write down what Jesus is saying to you. Remember his words will come as impressions to your mind, thoughts that will show up and are not ordinarily there."

Then Brian thought of the verse in Galatians 2:

I am crucified with Christ, nevertheless I live, and Christ lives in me.

In one sense he was up on that cross with Christ. Jesus' death was his death. And Brian knew that without death there would be no new life.

As Brian knelt there in that sacred space in silence before Jesus, he saw Jesus his shepherd dying for him as well as others. His shepherd was giving his life so that others could live, a sacrificial giving that brought life to others.

Brian thought of his three children, two boys and a girl who were not really involved at all with their Christian faith. He took them to Church, encouraged them to do what was right, but never was the spiritual leader in the home. "I left that to my wife," he said.

"As I was looking at Jesus on the cross, I decided I needed to join him and give my life for my children. I wanted them to experience the kind of walk with Jesus I was now discovering. In their religious upbringing I had never helped them to develop a relationship with Jesus Christ. It was CHURCH and not CHRIST - all about doing and not about being."

"I then asked Jesus, 'What do you want me to do to reach my children and bring them back to you?' Then I began to write. Jesus was giving me a plan to bring my children back to the faith."

"What did he say," I inquired.

"Jesus told me to love my children - really love them. I had neglected them for a number of years and, as I said, not been the spiritual leader of our home. So the first thing Jesus wanted me to do was to ask my children to forgive me for being a poor spiritual leader. Then he wanted me to pray specifically for my children each day - pray for their return to the faith.

Last, Jesus told me not to preach at them, but to live out the new life I was learning to live. The more I DEMONSTRATED Christ's love, the more they would be drawn to me and ultimately to the Jesus who is with me."

"Jesus also encouraged me to be a better leader at Church in bringing people there into a personal, daily, moment by moment relationship with Christ."

"That's great," I stated. "It sounds like you are becoming a Psalm 23 person - not only letting Jesus be your shepherd, but learning to be a shepherd to your family like Jesus is to you."

Last, we covered Brian's Day 5 with Psalm 23. You recall he was to get into his easy chair, to recline and rest in the arms of Jesus, letting the message of Psalm 23 sink deep into his heart.

Brian did this, having never done anything like it before. He related what happened.

"I sat in my recliner, reclined, made sure my mind was slowing down, and that I was truly resting in the arms of Jesus. All at once Jesus seemed to speak:

Brian, I am your shepherd and have been caring for you for decades. I love you, and you can count on my presence to be with you always. I am so thankful that you are taking more time to get to know me. Just relax now and let me hold you.

Brian said that he closed his eyes and sank deeply into the arms of Jesus. It was so comforting. He felt absolutely secure and at peace.

"It was awesome! I have never felt the presence of God in my life in such a concrete way. For some time I lay there in a state of perfect peace. I didn't say anything and neither did God. But there was no question that we were enjoying each other's presence. It was beautiful and lasted over 20 minutes. I guess this is what contemplation is - to be in the awesome presence of Jesus, drinking in his presence."

Then Brian summed it up.

"What a change in my life this past week as I spent time with Jesus in Psalm 23. I feel like I'm just beginning on a journey into the heart of God. And though I still miss my wife's presence, I'm beginning to realize the presence of Jesus, my LORD, my shepherd. He is always there waiting to have a conversation. My depression is subsiding, I have renewed hope because I have a friend with me at all times to dispel my loneliness. I'm actually beginning to love my life again as this new joy is beginning to grab hold of my inner soul."

Brian then went on talking.

"Dr. Paul, you have me hooked on journaling. What should I do to keep it up?"

"Brian, I'm so encouraged by what you have discovered this week and the relationship you are developing with Jesus. So here's an assignment to keep you going for next week."

"Brian, read John 15 prayerfully, only a few words at a time or a paragraph at most. Underline any words you think are important. Slow down your eyes - look, observe what the text is saying.

Sometimes I bombard the text with questions: why, what, when, how, where, who? Talk to Jesus about your questions and the words you underline. Sometimes I go to the dictionary or a thesaurus to see other words that are similar that will give me new insight. Peel the text back like you are peeling an onion. There are layers there. Go slow. You don't have to finish John 15 this week. Just begin."

I wrote out what I wanted Brian to do:

1. Read the Scripture (John 15) slowly, prayerfully
2. Underline any words you think are important
3. Use your eyes - look, write down your observations
4. Ask why, what, when, how, where, who?
5. Talk to Jesus about the questions you ask
6. Listen, interact with him, write it down
7. Always ask him what he wants you to do in response to the passage
8. End in praise and thanksgiving

As you read about what I shared with Brian, it would be good for you to to go to John 15 and work through this passage with Jesus by your side. He has things he wants to show you about yourself, about himself, about others.

Also, read about Lectio divina in the next chapter along with the chapter on the Five Questions to ask when reading Scripture. Then think through the chapter on the Rosary. These last few chapters on INTIMACY are meant to open new doors to you so that you will not only talk with God through prayer, but learn how to carry on a dialogue with him - a two way conversation that will greatly deepen your faith.

It will make all the difference!

CHAPTER 4

Lectio Divina

Lectio Divina is a slow, prayerful, meditative, contemplative approach to the Scriptures. Lectio Divina means "divine reading." It is a very old practice in the Church and goes back to St. Benedict in the 6th century. There are rules you must follow to practice Lectio Divina. It is an approach to Holy Scripture that is:

1. **SLOW.** You are not out to read an entire section, chapter or even a paragraph. You go word by word, drinking in the meaning, pausing as you observe this word of God to you. You don't want to miss anything. You have prayed: "Open my eyes that I may see wondrous things out of your word" (Psalm 119), and you believe that this will come to pass. You are centering on HIM, your creator, your master, your intimate friend.

It may take you a week, two weeks, a month to get through a chapter. But that's OK. It's not how much of the Bible you get through that counts but how much of the Bible gets into you. This is a treasure hunt where you are looking under every word for that special treasure God has for you. It is like squeezing an orange, desiring to get out all the juice, the sweetness into your soul. You are seeking to merge your thoughts with HIS thoughts. So you quiet your mind, find a place where you can leisurely loiter in the presence of the God who wants to embrace you, guide you, and be your friend.

59

2. **PRAYERFUL.** It is here in the Scriptures that we meet face to face with God. He wants to enfold us into a deep relationship with him. So we pray, "Come Father, come Holy Spirit, come Lord Jesus and meet me as I drink in your precious words." It is in this process that we find that Jesus will "open our minds to understand the Scriptures," like he did those early two disciples on the road to Emmaus. So as we read the Holy Scriptures, we are always praying, communicating with the God who gave us his word.

The Scriptures are like a telescope that bring us into the presence of God. Too often people study the telescope, take it apart, know all about how it functions and works. And that may be good, but the ultimate purpose of a telescope is to bring a person into the presence of the stars. So too the Scriptures. You can study them, memorize them, read them, tear them apart, but until you let them bring you into the presence of Jesus, you are not using them the way they were designed.

This is why, when we open this sacred book, we pray and keep on praying. The words of Scripture are not ordinary words. They are powerful, explosive, life changing. And we cannot come with human understanding and think we will grasp what these words mean. We must tune our ears to the writer of these words, God himself, talking with him, and letting him talk with us.

3. **MEDITATIVE.** Here we are ruminating, marinating, chewing, rolling over the words of Scripture in our minds and hearts. During this time we are talking with God and letting him talk with us. The "ears on our hearts" like Solomon, are attentive,

ready to receive insight, the kind that produces a "burning in our hearts," like it did on those two early disciples with Jesus. At this point we begin direct dialogue with God, interacting, drinking, eating, breathing in his words, letting our souls consume them, this spiritual nourishment that is vital to our spiritual existence. God is becoming our friend in an intimacy that cannot be described, so deep it is, so close, so loving. We share with him our deepest desires, our hopes, our dreams, our pain, our doubts, our confidence in him. And we listen, drinking in his words in the moment, *rhema,* hot bread for the soul that results in joy and inner gladness.

King David in Psalm 1, talks about ruminating on the Scriptures day and night. I recommend people memorize sections of Scriptures as they work through them, words of God that they can sift through in their minds and hearts through the day. Like a cow chewing its cud, we can chew on the Word of God, slowly, meditatively, getting out of it all the nourishment that is needed for that moment.

4. **CONTEMPLATIVE.** You are swept into a place of total reverence, praise and joy. You drink it in, not saying anything, not listening at this point, just lingering, resting in HIS presence. There is a total silence, yet a communication that goes beyond words taking us into infinity, into the realm of God, into his throne room, the holy of holies. It is like two lovers who embrace without saying any words. The moment has swept them into an encounter of their souls. So too with God. He is in us, we in him, in that infinite, finite embrace.

It is like mouth to mouth resuscitation. We receive his life. At this point we may hear the groans of the Holy Spirit that St. Paul talks about in Romans 8, uttering words that we cannot understand. It is awesome, breathtaking, magnificent, overwhelming and absolutely necessary if we are going to get back to the Garden of Eden where we lost this great gift, communing with and embracing our creator.

This brings about the change we need, a change that breathes into us - HIS life.

CHAPTER 5

THE FIVE QUESTIONS Method
TO READING THE SCRIPTURE
(Can be used with the daily readings)

When you read a specific Scripture or focus on the daily readings like The WORD Among Us, MAGNIFICAT, or others, ask the following five questions. They will help you to dig deeper and allow you to benefit greatly with your time with God. It is best to read a paragraph or two as you do this.

1. What is a KEY WORD, words or phrase that stands out when I read this passage? Look it up in the dictionary to get its clear meaning or use biblehub.com. (See appendix on how to use biblehub.com).

2. In a SENTENCE or two, what is the passage talking about?

3. Can I ILLUSTRATE what the passage is talking about in my own life or in the life of another?

4. What is Jesus ASKING ME TO DO in response to this passage?

5. If Jesus were standing before me right now (and he is!) and asked me: "**WHAT DO YOU WANT** me to do for you?" What would I say?

Write these answers down in your journal. It's life changing!

CHAPTER 6

USING THE ROSARY
AS AN AID TO LISTEN TO JESUS

The great thing about the Rosary is that it brings us to Jesus through his, and our   Blessed Mother, Mary. It is an awesome devotional when prayed with open eyes and ears, ready to interact with Jesus.

Here are some suggestions:

1. Slow down when you pray the Rosary. Jesus said that we are not to ramble through our prayers, saying them by rote, a repetition that is somehow mindless.

Pope Paul VI clearly points this out when he says:

> *Without contemplation, the Rosary is a body without a soul*, *and its recitation runs the risk of becoming a mechanical repetition of formulas, in violation of the admonition of Christ: 'In praying do not heap up empty phrases as the Gentiles do; for they think they will be heard for their many words (Matt. 6:7).'*

He goes on to say that:

*We should **make every effort to meditate on the mysteries** each and every time we pray the Rosary. The Rosary is no substitute for Lectio Divina; on the contrary, it presupposes and promotes it.*

For further insight read: John Paul II in his encyclical "Rosarium Virginis Mariae"

2. Pause at each meditation. Enter into it. Drink in its message...to YOU, TODAY. What does Jesus want you to do in response to this meditation? For example, as you pray through the *Sorrowful Mysteries,* Jesus may be asking you to carry the cross for someone today. Who might that be? How does he want you to do it? Write this in your journal.

Or you may be praying through the *Joyful Mysteries* and find Jesus asking you to be more open to his grace, or that you should "give birth" to Jesus in such a way that others see Jesus in you through your love, your care, your generosity. You might even ask: "To whom, Jesus, do you want me to show yourself today - your grace, your love?"

And then as you meditate on the *Luminous Mysteries,* you may pause at the transfiguration and ask Jesus: "Where do you want me to be that glowing light today? To whom?" Use the Rosary to interact with God. Don't let it be just a one way street where you talk with God - a monologue. Make it a dialogue.

Pray, listen, obey.

And enjoy the fruit of this relationship.

PART 2

MISSION

A LOVE FOR....*OTHERS*

CHAPTER 1

MEN LIVING *ON PURPOSE*

St. Paul was quite a guy. In his day he had traveled the core of the world, planting Churches in the Mediterranean region. In fact someone said about him that "he had turned the world upside down with this Christian message."

Imagine that, turning the world upside down. Quite an accomplishment!

What moved him? Why was he so successful?

In Acts 20, not long before St. Paul was arrested and then spent years in jail because of his Christian faith, he said these riveting words:

> *My life means nothing except that I might finish the course, **the mission** given to me by Jesus Christ.*

The MISSION. That was it. That was why St. Paul was so successful. He had a mission that drove him. He lived life...ON PURPOSE. Everything he did was INTENTIONAL.

I had coffee with Todd some years ago. He seemed to be struggling and wanted my insight.

"What's up," I inquired?

"I'm not sure, " he shrugged. "It's just that I seem to be living in a fog. I go to work, come home, watch TV, drink a beer, kiss the wife, say 'hi' to the kids, go to Church and do that week after week, month after month, year after year. I seem to be loosing touch with the kids, my wife and I will never get a divorce, but the sizzle is gone in our marriage. I make good money at work, but professionally I'm at a stand still. And Church is OK, but frankly as I look at life...I'm bored."

> *Round and round and round*
> *We go*
> *Where we stop*
> *Nobody knows.*

Todd was not living life INTENTIONALLY. He was drifting without a focus, a purpose, a MISSION. And that equals...boredom.

So I gave him a mission that all men should have. They can be tweaked and personalized to fit their situation, but all men should INTENTIONALLY focus on these things.

72

CHAPTER 2

THEY NEED TO TAKE BACK
THEMSELVES
AND BRING THEIR LIVES UNDER
SUBMISSION TO CHRIST

Todd was like so many men...living not on purpose. He was like a billiard ball, being shot around the table by circumstances that seemed out of his control. Life was controlling him. He was not in control of his life. He was coasting day to day without intentionally living his life.

On Tuesday and Friday, when one prays the Rosary, the focus is on the "Sorrowful Mysteries." The first mystery is Christ in the garden where we see him praying: "Not my will but thine be done." What Jesus had to face, to bear the sin of the world was unthinkable. But he bowed his will to the will of his Father in absolute submission.

As I sat with Todd, I wondered if he would be willing to submit himself totally to the will and purpose of God. Would he say: "Not my will but thine be done."

And I ask you: "Are you willing to put you life under total submission to Christ and to discover the mission he has for you and your family?"

If you say, "No," then I feel sorry for you. You will waste your life on things, on aspirations that will not outlive you, and possibly lose your kids who will live like you do, lives full of emptiness, always seeking life but never really finding it.

But if you say, "Yes," then you are ready for the ride of your life! YOU have the possibility of TURNING YOUR WORLD UPSIDE DOWN and making such a difference that it will amaze those around you. You will become a Saint that LIVES ON PURPOSE, INTENTIONALLY with a MISSION that will move many into the Kingdom of God, including your family, friends, work associates, neighbors, relatives, and beyond…to a world that is looking for a man who will live his Catholic faith INTENTIONALLY.

In the book of Ezekiel, a prophet in the Old Testament, God came to him and said:

> *I am looking and searching for a MAN who will set up a wall of protection, a MAN to **stand in the gap** before me and his family, his relatives, his work associates, his neighbors, the world where he lives, that they would not be destroyed and experience hell in this life and the life to come, but find life in me. BUT I FOUND NONE.*
>
> Ezekiel 22:30 expanded

Those are somber words, aren't they?

God is looking for "GAP MEN," Catholic men who will live their Catholic faith INTENTIONALLY, ON PURPOSE, men with a MISSION. These men will be husbands who stand in the gap for their wives, fathers who stand in the gap for their children, men who will stand in the gap for their work associates, their neighbors, their relatives and the world.

Who is doing that today? Do you know of any? God is looking for someone. Will you be that man? St. Paul was that kind of a guy, a man on a mission. And the world is not the same because he was willing to stand in the gap, to be a MAN ON A MISSION.

If you want to be that man, pray with me this prayer.

> *Dear God,*
> *I'm not sure what to do, but I do know this, that I have not lived my Catholic faith INTENTIONALLY, I have not stood in the gap for my family and others. So, dear God, today, I am offering myself as a **GAP**man, to stand in the gap, to live my faith INTENTIONALLY, to learn about what I am to do for you and to do it, to accomplish this MISSION you have given me. And I do it trusting in your strength and guidance. Amen.*

Todd bowed his head and prayed that prayer. He wanted to be a **GAP**man, to live ON PURPOSE, INTENTIONALLY; to be a man with a MISSION. What happened was amazing. He began to experience a life that few men experience.

Todd started a movement that literally impacted thousands of other men....and families. As he began to live INTENTIONALLY each day, his world changed. Oh he still came home, had a beer, and watched his favorite sports teams. He was still a guy, but a guy who lived on PURPOSE.

He started a BEER & Bible FELLOWSHIP...a place where guys came, had a beer and talked about their faith. And the discussions were real, facing real issues men face about their jobs, their sexuality, money issues, sports, and their hopes and dreams.

Todd became a **GAP**man. And he produced many others.

A few years ago, Todd passed away at a good old age. The Church was packed with thousands of other souls who had been impacted by this man who lived life ON PURPOSE, with a MISSION to change his world for the glory of Christ.

Dozens of people gave a short testimony to the impact of Todd's life on them. They remembered when he was just a guy, an ordinary, Church going guy who did not have a mission. Then something happened. He found his purpose. He began to live intentionally. And now at the close of his life, he had made his life count for Jesus Christ. He wasn't just a guy anymore, but a guy who submitted his life to the MISSION of impacting his world.

I remember the day I challenged Todd to step out. Now a few decades later what a difference! God was saying to him:

Well done good and faithful servant. You have been faithful in a few things, I will set you over many things. Enter into the joy of my kingdom.

Matthew 25:21

What will God say to you when you die? Did you just take up space in your big chair drinking beer and not make an impact for Jesus Christ and his Kingdom?

The challenge is to either take up space or STAND IN A SPECIAL PLACE - being a **GAP**man - a man on PURPOSE, INTENTION-ALLY driven toward a MISSION - a special calling from God to impact your world.

Pray the prayer that Todd prayed. Keep reading how to be an IM-PACT MAN, and watch God work. You are about ready to enter into a kind of life that you never thought imaginable.

So grab a beer and keep reading!

CHAPTER 3

THEY NEED TO TAKE BACK THEIR *FAMILIES* AND BRING THEM UNDER THE LORDSHIP OF CHRIST

M en are the CEO's of their families. In Ephesians 5, St. Paul said that the husband is the HEAD of the wife and is to love her as Christ loved the Church. Being the head does not mean you can be bossy and a tyrant. What it means is that you are the SPIRITUAL LEADER and you do this INTENTIONALLY.

You see, many men leave the spiritual leadership to the wives. They go to Church and that's about it. Todd had done this much of his married life. He had never been the spiritual leader in his home. He did not realize that marriage is a Sacrament, and living out our marriage sacramentally is our holy duty and privilege.

A broad study a few years ago in the Anglican Church in England found that when the wife was the spiritual leader in the home, around 3% to 5% of the children continued on with the faith. But when the husband, the father, was the spiritual leader of the home, over 60% of the children were impacted by their faith and continued to live it out.

WOW!

If that doesn't grab you, nothing else will. Husbands and dads, you need to be the spiritual leader of your home. That's one of the INTENTIONAL things you do. This is part of your MISSION if you are going to be an IMPACT MAN.

How do you do this?

Todd was interested when I first showed him how to be an IMPACT man.

There are good books you can find that help you in the areas of loving your wife and your children, helping them to become Saints so they will go to heaven and not perish with those who do not receive Jesus and follow him. Do a Google search. Look up dads.org, christianfathers.com, catholicdadsonline.org, for example.

Or better yet, download the materials from crossingthegoal.com. This is a great Catholic ministry to men with fantastic materials that will encourage your faith, and help you to be a better man, a better father, a better husband. All of their materials are free - the lectures, the study materials. I encourage you to check out this site and use these great assets to become an IMPACT Man.

There are good Catholic books that can be of great help with your marriage and raising children. Look online or ask your pastor.

So your MISSION for your family is ultimately to help them to become SAINTS.

How does this happen?

To produce saints, you need to know how saints act. Here is a small list that will help.
Saints:

- **Pray** - they commune with God. Teach your family to do this

- **Read and meditate on the Scriptures**. Teach them Lectio Divina. A young child can learn how to do this. It's exciting to see a young mind listen to God and hear his voice. It's the essence of Christianity - the sheep hearing the voice of Jesus.

- **Pray the Rosary and do it intentionally - not just by rote**. They spend time on the mysteries, meditating on them, drinking them into their souls.

- **Spend time before the Blessed Sacrament**. They go to the Adoration Room and spend time with Jesus, drinking in his presence, his life. What an impact this can have on your children if you take them as they see their dad kneel before Jesus in humble reverence.

- **Go often to Mass** - taking in the life of Jesus in the Eucharist

- **Understand the value of the sacrament of Reconciliation**, confessing their sins and finding forgiveness, direction and freedom. Why not go as a family. Help your children not to fear but rather to embrace this great sacrament.

• **Love people.** They are generous with their money, their time and talents in their service of Christ. Enlist your children in the decision of giving money to the Church or other charities. This helps them to develop a spirit of charity and experience the joy of giving. Help them to do this with their own money too.

After Todd decided to be a GAPman, to live life ON PURPOSE, INTENTIONALLY, he wanted me to help him with his family.

We first focused on his WIFE.

We turned to Ephesians 5 where St. Paul COMMANDS husbands to love their wives as Christ loved the Church, giving himself up for her. I asked Todd: "Does your wife know, absolutely, that you love her?"

"I don't know. I tell her once in a while."

I went on to tell Todd how important it is for husbands to communicate with their wives, to be open, vulnerable, transparent. It's easy to be just a tough guy, drink beer, and do everything we can to not to be open and communicative.

I recall, years ago, when I was counseling a couple who were having marriage problems. They were fairly new Christians and needed a lot of help to save their marriage. The husband was a successful professional who at one time was an All American football player at one of the top universities in America. He was tough!

And that was the problem. He was still a jock. His wife needed a loving husband, not just a jock.

So, after a few sessions where I helped him understand the kind of husband God wanted him to be, I asked him to pray with his wife - to hold her hand and talk with God together. He said he would do it.

The next week when he came in for his counseling session, I asked him if he did his homework assignment.

This tough guy looked at me and said, sheepishly, "No. I just couldn't do it."

Here was an All American who didn't have the guts to pray with his wife.

Amazing!

But that's the story of most guys. We don't want to be open on the spiritual level with our wives. We keep that tough exterior that keeps them out of the center of who we are. They feel shut out, and ultimately unloved in a way their hearts long to be loved.

It was a few weeks later that this All American finally worked up the nerve to pray with his wife. When he told me what he accomplished it was as if he had climbed Mount Everest, or won the Super Bowl. This was one of his greatest achievements!

Later I helped him draw up a special calendar, a calendar entitled: *30 DAYS TO MAKING MY WIFE FEEL LIKE A SPECIAL PERSON.* If you want to know more about how to draw up this calendar and what to put in it, go to amazon.com and look up the book, *30 DAYS TO MAKING YOUR WIFE FEEL LIKE A SPECIAL PERSON.*

This calendar included special things he would say to his wife, surprising her with notes on the mirror, flowers, special dates, etc. He was creative and came up with a good calendar. Most of all, he sought to help his wife feel significant and secure.

After he spent this special 30 days, pleasing his wife, doing special things for her, he came to my office with a big smile. He felt like a million dollars. And his marriage was changing for the good as he took the leadership in loving his wife as Christ loved the Church, a love that was sacrificial, giving, total.

For a tough football player, he was doing great. Tough is good. But with the wife, tender is better…always!

Then there are the children. To be the spiritual leader of the home means that, as we said before, your goal is to get them to heaven in grand style. Saints are what it's all about. So that means a lot of discipline for you as well as for them. You will need to discipline your time and set spiritual goals for them. What should they know? How can they get to know God more fully and have a daily, personal relationship with him?

A lot of the discipline is really discipleship. The word discipline comes from the word disciple - and that's what we want from our sons and daughters - to disciple them so that they will have a mature walk with Jesus. Often when we have behavioral problems we need to look at ways to better disciple them. It is easy to punish children when they get out of line.

But the better tactic is to ask yourself: "What do I need to do to help them learn how to act more in line with a saint." And by saint I am not talking about being a "goody two-shoes." When I raised my sons I wanted them to be true men, leaders, going for broke for God, fearless, faithful men, not a bunch of sissy Christians. I wanted them to have a "fire in their belly," to be bold in their faith - no "arm chair" Christians.

One thing I do now with my sons and daughter, their wives and husbands as well as our 14 grandchildren is to pray the Rosary for them at least 7 days a week. In so doing I not only say the "Hail Mary full of grace..." but spend the bulk of my time praying through the mysteries for each of my family. On each of the mysteries I focus on, each one of the five I lift up my family, thinking of all of them, praying for them that they might experience the fullness of that mystery - and live it out fully in their lives.

In one sense, I am praying the Rosary ON PURPOSE. I have a MISSION in mind as I pray it. There is INTENTION. And the result is that Mary hears me, the Saints hear me, Jesus hears me, and PRAYER DOES CHANGE THINGS...AND PEOPLE, even your family.

If you would like to see how I pray through the Rosary for my family, look up on <u>amazon.com</u> my book on this subject, *I'm Praying The Rosary For YOU!* It's a book you will use not only for yourself, but send to those you are praying for. It will not only change them, but you in the process.

Last, there is another thing you can do as the spiritual leader. Live out the acronym, L.O.V.E.

L - **isten** to each member of the family - your wife and children. Too often men are not good listeners and because of that your wife and children do not feel valued. Listen with your ears and eyes. Watch. Be aware of what is happening. It is so easy to talk *at* our wife or children and not *with* them, pausing, listening, asking questions, seeking their ideas, watching for words that come from the heart.

O - **ptimistic**. Be cheerful, positive, not a grump. You are the leader and know where you are taking the family. When problems arise, you know what to do because of your relationship with Jesus. He is your Commander and Chief. With Christ as your leader, you will always be moving towards victory.

V - **igilant**. Be vigilant. You have an enemy that wants to destroy your family. The world headed up by Satan is out to corrupt your family, to neutralize it, even break it apart. Be watchful. Read Ephesians 6 about spiritual warfare. And read I Peter 5 where our first Pope talks about Satan being like a lion, seeking to devour us. You must guard your children from worldly attachments and help them to find true life in Christ. Don't close your eyes and think they can't get hurt. Satan is out to destroy your family. Watch. Beware. And know that he doesn't stand a chance as long as you wear your armor (see Ephesians 6).

E - **quip** them to be saints. What skills do they need to learn? What information is important? Teach. Train. And then reap the great fruit of your work.

I have devised a teaching program you could go through as a family entitled, *KNOW WHAT YOU BELIEVE - A Dynamic Catechism For Today*. It can help each member of the family to be able to talk about their faith and what they believe, in a very learnable, teachable plan. You can get it on amazon.com.

When you live INTENTIONALLY this way, you will then have confidence that God will be with you. And your family will greatly benefit.

> *Train up a child in the way he should go.*
> *And when he is old he will not depart from it.*
> Proverbs 22:6

> *Fathers, do not provoke your children to anger, but bring them up with the training and instruction of the Lord.*
> Ephesians 6:4

CHAPTER 4

THEY NEED TO TAKE BACK
THEIR *CHURCH*

Your Catholic Church needs to be brought under the full and total authority of the Catholic Church. So many Catholic Churches have drifted. They have lost their MISSION of making saints of those who come and of all those who have fallen away, as well as everyone else in your parish.

There are too many Priests who are not GAP men. Why? They want to be liked. They want to fit in. Or they disagree with Catholic teaching. So they carry out the Sacraments (thank God), but very little else. They have lost their passion for ministry, for impacting their world.

On the other side, there are many dedicated Priests who follow Christ fully and have a passion for souls, who see their parish as a mission field, a place to reach the lost, bring back fallen away Catholics, and to help all Catholics to become Saints.

As you seek to take back your Church, let me ask you a question: How many people live in your parish? 10,000? 20,000? Many are on their way to a godless eternity unless we reach them with the good news of the Gospel. We feed the poor, and we should.

We march for the unborn, and more should do that. But who is going to the people who live within the borders of the parish and reaching them. Their souls are in jeopardy. It is far worse than dying due to lack of food. They are spiritually dying for lack of the bread that brings eternal life - Jesus Christ.

But few, if anyone, are doing anything. Those who come within the shelter of our Church are fed. The rest can go to hell!...at least that's the way we are acting. Who cares? The Church is to be a lighthouse in that parish - bringing Jesus to the families who live there.

Imagine with me for a moment a house that is on fire, and five family members live there. As you walk by the home you see the flames begin to leap from the roof. They are in danger! So what do you do?

Walk by?

Oh, you don't want to be troubled. You don't know the family and don't want to disturb them. They may be eating dinner or watching TV.

NO! You would never do that!

Then why, when people's souls are in jeopardy, do we walk by, not wanting to bother them. Where is our Christian love? So we sit in our Churches with the world around us, all those families in our parish, many fallen away Catholics, and WE DON'T CARE. The proof of our lack of concern is that we are doing nothing to save them.

In 20 years the Catholic Church will be half the size. The older generation is dying. And the new generation is no longer involved. But this can change. If you will be an INTENTIONAL Catholic, a man with a MISSION, you can have an impact on your Church. Gather some other men. Start IMPACT groups. Include your pastor if he wants to participate. But you be the leader. Carry out this IMPACT MAN program. Stand in the gap. And watch as exciting things begin to happen.

Oh yes, you may not find help from your pastor. He may feel intimated by what you are doing. But move ahead in a spirit of love, generosity and prayer. Let him be the pastor. You move ahead and be an IMPACT MAN - at home, in your Church, in your community.

And I have another goal as you take back your Church. As you form IMPACT GROUPS, I encourage each group to have as their goal finding a young man who will consider going to seminary and becoming a priest. The goal would be to have each group find one man each year. Imagine what would happen in your diocese if groups of men were always on the lookout for more priests. This can happen first in your home as your raise your sons to desire this special place of service as well as your daughters who would look favorably at the religious life. This INTENTIONAL MISSION could produce hundreds of godly, powerful young people who would serve the Church. This alone would be revolutionary!

And that's what we want to start…

A REVOLUTION!

If you are a Priest or Bishop who is reading this book, imagine what would happen if you decided to be an IMPACT man in your Church and diocese. Pay special attention to the section on the commitment to building in the lives of other men and the impact that could make - a revolutionary impact.

CHAPTER 5

THEY NEED TO TAKE BACK
THEIR *WORKPLACE*

This is an awesome mission field that is untapped today. You have relationships with people who need Christ. Their souls long for fulfillment. They are hungry for a purpose that is beyond themselves. And you have the answer - a relationship with Jesus Christ.

But how do you reach your work associates?

As you begin, ask God whom you should focus on first. He may give you a name or two. Then begin to pray specifically for each of them, that God would open a door of opportunity for you to share your faith.

There are good books that will help you learn how to share your faith. A few good books you could read would be *Evangelizing Catholics* by Scott Hahn, and *How To Share your Faith With Anyone* by Terry Barber. Or you can read one I wrote entitled, *You Can Change Your World*. It covers material that will show you how to begin to change your world in 100 days. You can purchase it on amazon.com.

Above all, use love. Don't be preachy, but also, don't be afraid to TALK about your faith. Living it in front of your work associates and being willing to discuss it as well as standing up for Catholic teaching and morality is a vital part of your mission. As you stand up, be clear, loving, helping people to get into a dialogue that seeks to be informational and educational.

Too often emotions get in the way. There may be gays who are married, or a young woman who just had an abortion. The goal is not to condemn, but to help your associates understand that if there is a creator, God, and if he has given us a manual on how best to live our lives, isn't it best that we follow it? And if this God loves us, and he does, he proved it by sending his Son to die for us, won't he then want to give us the best?

Of course!

Does a child know what is best for it or does the parent? If God is our father, our parent, should we follow what we want, our desires as children, or what he desires?

Try to help people think. Everyone has their own life preserver that they are trusting in as they live their lives. Only when they see that their life preserver has a gaping hole in it will they consider the one you have, Jesus Christ and the eternal life he offers, life that is full and abundant.

Smile. Don't be a Pharisee. But be bold. Be confident. Be loving.

And you will have a great impact on the job.

Todd took this advice and began to see a few of his associates become Catholics, as well as seeing other Catholics who had fallen away come back to the faith.

Todd also did another thing. He began to see that his real boss was God, not the one who gave him a paycheck. He concluded this from the passage St. Paul wrote in Colossians:

*Employees, obey your employers in everything, not only when being watched, as currying favor, but in simplicity of heart, fearing the Lord. **Whatever you do, do from the heart, as for the Lord who is your real boss**, and not for others. In so doing you will receive an eternal payment from God as you see yourself enslaved to Jesus Christ and him alone.*

Colossians 3:22-24 Expanded

Not only did Todd see God as his real boss, but he also began to see his work as a ministry. Like a Priest is called to pastor a Church, Todd began to realize that he too was called to be a priest (the common priesthood of believers) at work.

He happened to be a financial advisor and helped hundreds invest their money. It was kind of a ho-hum job until he realized that he was not just a financial advisor but a priest, a minister that could help people find their true purpose for money - provide for their families, others and the kingdom of God. When he realized this, his job took on new meaning. Everyday he got up with a prayer on his heart, "God, help me to help people to not trust their money but you. May I nudge people in the right direction to see that they can't ultimately trust in WHAT they have but rather in WHO they have - a God who loves them and will take care of them."

This changed Todd and his work, a work that took on a new dimension. It was now HIS MINISTRY. He was there to help people discover the true value of money, and to ultimately find the life they really wanted and desired, a security tied up in a God who loved them and wanted the best for them.

Todd also challenged many to move from being takers to being givers, investing in the kingdom of God. It was amazing. Every day he got up with a zeal for his work - his ministry. No longer was it a job, the ho-hum of daily work, the boredom, the monotony, the daily grind. He had a purpose, and intention, a mission to accomplish, not just for himself or for his company, but for God.

No matter what kind of job you have, God is your boss, and he has placed you in that work to accomplish a ministry. Pray about what it is and how to carry it out in the power of the Holy Spirit.

Like Todd, all you are seeking to do is to help people to become IMPACT people, to find God in an INTIMATE way, to develop a God given MISSION, to be a person that experiences the POWER that comes through Purity and holiness, to be ANCHORED in the faith, COMMITTED to other people and to live life TRIUMPHANTLY, not in the lack luster and boredom so many experience.

CHAPTER 6

THEY NEED TO TAKE BACK
THEIR
NEIGHBORHOOD AND COMMUNITY

As Todd grew in his faith he began to realize that the people across the street, next door, down three doors, need Christ. Their souls are longing for something that this world cannot fill. You have the answer.

Up to this time, Todd had been a   SECRET SERVICE CHRISTIAN - only God knew for sure!

Here's a few things Todd learned.

Lovingly embrace your neighbors with generosity and kindness. Have a block party. Get to know them. Pray for them each day. Be open to circumstances where you can talk about your faith. If there is a serious need, pray WITH them.

YOU ARE A PRIEST TO YOUR NEIGHBORS!

You can say something like this: "Do you mind if I pray for you right now and ask for God's help?"

Most people HAVE NEVER been prayed for. They have never heard their name mentioned in prayer. Again, read *YOU CAN CHANGE YOUR WORLD* for some more helps on what you can do to reach your neighborhood.

Could you reach one neighbor a year for Christ? What would you need to do to accomplish that? And what would your neighborhood look like in 10 years after you have reached 10 families for Christ - families who are now going to your Church, involved, loving Jesus and having an impact in the neighborhood, workplace, and beyond.

WOW!

Talk about impact.

Then your life will count. You won't be just another Catholic man who goes home from work, opens a can of beer and watches a ball game. By the time you die there could be thousands who have been impacted by your life and by the God you love and serve.

You will be living ON PURPOSE, with a MISSION, INTENTIONALLY being the man God desires, a...

GAPman.

Standing in the gap, and making a difference for eternity.

PART 3

POWER OF PURITY

LOVING...*YOURSELF*

CHAPTER 1

NO POWER
WITHOUT PURITY

What is purity?

Too often we think purity has to do with sexual purity. We will talk about that in the next few chapters. But first, think of this. When you drink water, you want it to be pure, don't you? If you see any strange things floating around in your glass, you will probably dump it out. So if you desire purity, don't you think God does?

Of course!

Heaven is a PERFECT place. God will not let anyone in who is not perfect.

The problem: **SIN SOILS**
The solution: **CHRIST CLEANSES**

I recall talking to a man whom I was seeking to lead to Christ. One day during breakfast he told me how good he was, that he lived by the golden rule and wasn't a drunk, a lier or a thief. I congratulated him and then said: "But that's not good enough. To get into heaven you have to be perfect."

"Perfect!" he exclaimed, somewhat shocked. "No one is perfect."

I took a glass of water that was on the table, and said: "Let's say this glass of water is heaven - a perfect place where God lives." I then took the pepper on the table and began to shake it over the water in the glass. "What is happening to the water," I asked? "It's getting messed up," he said. I agreed and then said: "That's what happens if you try to put us in heaven if we are not perfect. Heaven get's messed up, and God can't allow that. So we MUST BE PERFECT if we are going to get into heaven, absolutely pure."

"Then none of us can make it," he said.

"That's the bad news," I said. "It was Jesus who said that we had to *be perfect even as God the Father is perfect.* God demands total and complete holiness. But there is very GOOD NEWS. Jesus Christ takes our imperfections and gives us his perfection. It's what St. Paul said when he wrote to the Corinthians:"

> *He who knew no sin became sin for us that WE MIGHT BE-*
> *COME THE RIGHTEOUSNESS OF GOD IN HIM.*
> II Corinthians 5:21

"In other words, at our baptism Jesus takes all our sin, all our imperfections, all our impurity and washes them away. And he continues to do that when we confess our sins on a daily basis as well as practice the Sacrament of Reconciliation."

This friend of mine finally saw his need for purity, was baptized and took the steps to live a life of purity.

So, we see the need and value of purity. Jesus said in the Beatitudes (Matthew 5):

Blessed (or joyful) are the pure in heart for they shall see God.

Purity is vitally important. One reason you change the oil in your car is that gunk gets into it and, if you don't change it, your car will have major problems. So too with us. We need to get the gunk out of our lives.

How do we do this?

I am not going into it in detail. Look online at *examination of conscience*. This will get you started. Many Catholics do this every night just before they go to sleep. Others do it once a week. But the important thing is this - get rid of the gunk - those sins that you struggle with, those sins that easily distract you (see Hebrews 12:1).

Let me list some sins or weaknesses that lead to sin so you can see which ones you struggle with the most. These sins (or weaknesses) are like small little people that ride on our shoulders and keep whispering into our ears, sins (or weaknesses) that are the most common in our lives. They are normally venial sins that we struggle with like impatience (a form of anger), or judgmentalism (there is a place for right judgment, but judmentalism is when we are too often focusing on what is wrong rather than what is right. We become the judge and jury and pronounce others guilty. When we do that we often lack the grace, mercy and love of God).

Remember, without purity there is no power. The gunk in our lives will keep us from having the kind of Christian influence that we should have as men.

Even anxiety and restlessness can move from being a weakness to a sin. Saint Augustine said: "You have made us for yourself, O Lord, and our heart is restless until it rests in you." So you see the need to rest in God. It was Solomon who said:

> *Trust in the LORD with all your heart and lean not on your own understanding...* Proverbs 3:5

Yet we too often lean on our own understanding, don't we? We fret, worry, and are full of anxiety when God wants us to more fully trust him.

Though you can look at sins seen under the umbrella of the 10 Commandments (see the great materials in the Catechism of the Catholic Church), for this book I am going to list some sins (or weaknesses) that are normative among Catholic men. It's a good list to begin with.

It might be a good idea too, when you journal, to ask God what sins are most prevalent in your life. Then wait. The Holy Spirit will highlight some. Confess these and get cleaned up! Walk under the cleansing showers of God's grace!

On the next few pages are a list of some of the sins (some may be weaknesses that can easily become sins) that need to be dealt with. Go slow enough to see if you need to confess that sin and find forgiveness.

Also, we not only confess the things that we DID but also the things WE FAILED TO DO. Think of all the good God asked you to do but failed to do it, the smile, that gracious act, that loving response, being quiet when you should have spoken up. Hundreds of things that go undone. This too is sin, impurity that gunks up our lives.

Confess it all. Come clean. Practice the Sacrament of Reconciliation. And God will smile!

As you look at this list of sins, ask: "Is this a sin that I have committed? Is it a weakness that too often becomes a sin?" And most important, ask: **"Would Jesus Christ be doing this?"** We are ultimately to walk as he walked, to think and act like he thought and acted. The goal is to be CHRISTians, Christ in us to the point where we think his thoughts and do his actions.

Of course we fail. Yet, there is a remedy for that failure, the forgiveness of our Savior who gave himself for us, and gives us the strength to have victory over our sin.

Realize this, that most of us as men do not have problems with scrupulosity (An overly scrupulous conscience is an exaggeration of healthy guilt which then becomes unhealthy and causes great anxiety). Instead, we make EXCUSES for our sins instead of making CONFESSION.

Read this list. Pray about it. See what the Holy Spirit is saying to you. Then confess to God and before a Priest. Come clean. Aim for purity.

If the sin you have is a MORTAL SIN - a sin that is 1) grave, 2) with full knowledge that it is mortal and 3) you do it willfully with full knowledge, then rush to the Church and confess this sin to a Priest.

VENIAL SINS are slight sins. They do not break our friendship with God, although they injure it. They too need to be confessed so that one can be forgiven and made right before God.

If you have a weakness, you do not need to confess that - it is a weakness. But if that weakness weakens you to the point to where you sin, then confess that.

For example, let's say that you are prone to anxiety. Anxiety itself is not a sin unless you shut God out of the picture and don't bring him into your anxiety and worry. Anger is not always a sin. It is a healthy response to injustice. But if it sits and sours, it leads to bitterness and resentment resulting in outbursts of rage. Then, it is sin.

Here is a list of the *Seven Deadly or Capital Sins* with expanded lists under each. Read this slowly and put a mark by the sins that you struggle with the most. You can use this list when you see your priest for confession. It's a great aid.

PRIDE (The opposite of HUMILITY) Pride is the excessive belief in one's own abilities and interferes with your recognition of the grace of God. It has been called the sin from which all others arise. Notice the middle letter in pride - prIde. That says it all, being "I" centered and not God and other centered. Here are a few sins we can place under pride.

- Boastful
- Conceited
- Unbelief
- Lack of humility
- Domineering
- Lack of prayer (basically living like you don't need God)
- Anxiety that is based on self trust and not turning to God for help
- Manipulative
- Narcissism
- Racism
- Self-willed
- Arrogant
- Self righteous
- Thinking I'm better than others
- Failure to be a good listener
- Lack of gratitude
- Judgmental (critical spirit)
- Complacent
- Ego centered
- Self-sufficiency that lacks trust in others and God

- Aloofness
- Conceited
- Pompous
- Swagger
- Contemptuousness
- Little time for God (me focused)
- Knowingly making a bad confession
- Lying to protect yourself
- Deception, protecting a false image of yourself or what you are doing

ENVY (The opposite of LOVE) Envy is the desire for what other people have, their traits, status, abilities or situation.
- Covetousness
- Jealous
- Malice
- Prejudice
- Resentment
- Backbiting
- Gossip
- Spite
- Lust after things, position, status, someone's affection
- Contempt of others
- Slander

GLUTTONY (The opposite of TEMPERANCE) Gluttony is an inordinate desire to consume more than what you require - food, money, resources.
- Overeating
- Failure to FAST like I should

- Overspending
- Excess
- Unrestraint
- Sensuality
- Craving (always without being full)
- Lust for food, things
- Always hungry for more
- Dissipation
- Drunk
- Intemperance
- Orgy (consuming huge amounts of food and drink)
- Overindulgence
- Binge
- Insatiableness

LUST (The opposite of CHASTITY) Lust is the inordinate craving for pleasures of your body.
- Lover of pleasure more than a lover of God
- Pornography
- Masturbation
- Inappropriate sexual thoughts, fantasies
- Artificial birth control
- Incest
- Adultery
- Drug addiction
- Flirtatious
- Homosexual practice
- Orgy (wild sexual escapades)
- Sensuality
- Lewdness

- Carouse
- Fornication
- Seduction
- Sexual addiction
- Telling dirty, sexually debasing jokes
- Curiosity (a lust to know what I don't need to know)
- Voyeurism - seeking to see what should be private

ANGER - **Wrath or Rage** (The opposite of MEEKNESS) Anger is when you spurn love and opt instead for fury, wrath, at times expressing a temper.
- Bitterness
- Resentment
- Revenge - get even
- Murder
- Hate
- Cursing
- Filthy speech
- Impatience that leads to self oriented anger
- Griping, complaining (a habit)
- Political anger and discussion that leads nowhere
- Un-forgiveness
- Violence
- Fume (anger that is suppressed - that inward feeling of annoyance)
- Antagonize
- Moody (inwardly upset and focused on self)
- Feeling sorry for yourself (angry at someone else or event)
- Abuse of wife, children and others
- Pessimism (seeing most things as bad and upset about it)

- Stubborn
- Using four letter words inappropriately

GREED (The opposite of LIBERALITY) Greed is the desire for money, material wealth and goods. It is the sin of excess. It is sometimes called covetousness.
- Love of money
- Love of things
- Crooked business tactics
- Hoarding
- Stealing
- Selfishness
- Stingy
- Wasting money
- Not laying up treasure in heaven
- Insatiableness (never satisfied, content)
- Selfish craving
- Sensuality
- Unscrupulousness
- Lack of gratitude
- Cheating

SLOTH (The opposite of DILIGENCE)   Sloth is the avoidance of physical or spiritual work.
- Laziness
- Slow obedience (taking too long to obey)
- Wasting time
- Goof off (too much!)
- Inactivity
- Lethargy

- Do nothingness
- Not loving my wife as Christ loved the Church
- Not loving God with all my heart, soul, mind and strength
- Not loving my neighbor as myself
- Not spiritually leading my family (wife, children, grandchildren)
- Not taking care of my body (eating, sleeping, resting, exercise)
- Not practicing the presence of God
- Not listening to God - developing "ears on my heart."
- Rushing my time with God - it becomes a thing to do, not a person to be with
- Lack of love for the lost (those who do not know Christ)
- Missed Mass deliberately
- Lack of respect and honor to my parents
- Lackadaisicalness - Showing no interest, vigor, determination, or enthusiasm.
- Spiritual coma
- Inaction
- Impassivity
- Spiritual laziness
- Too lazy to practice the seven capital and spiritual virtues (chastity, abstinence, generosity, diligence, patience, kindness and humility)
- Negligence
- Sponger (being a taker instead of a giver)
- Idler
- Apathy
- Lack of tenderness and understanding (not fully loving)

- Receiving the Eucharist with known mortal sin but too lazy to do anything about it
- Making a bad confession
- Not defending my faith
- Not living life on purpose, intentionally, with a mission

If you want to study these seven deadly sins in more depth, look up *crossingthegoal.com*. Go to their study of the Seven Deadly Sins. There will be videos on each one as well as a study guide. I highly recommend this site.

To look at a list of sins in another way, notice these six biblical lists and let the Holy Spirit nudge you as to which ones that you struggle with the most. They are not exhaustive. There are other sins mentioned elsewhere in the Bible.

1 Corinthians 6:9-10

*Or do you not know that **wrongdoers** will not inherit the kingdom of God? Do not be deceived: Neither the **sexually immoral** nor **idolaters** nor **adulterers** nor **homosexual offenders**, nor **thieves** nor the **greedy** nor **drunkards** nor **slanderers** nor **swindlers** will inherit the kingdom of God. And that is what some of you were.*

Galatians 5:19-21

*The acts of the flesh are obvious: **sexual immorality, impurity** and **debauchery; idolatry** and **witchcraft; hatred, discord, jealousy**, fits of **rage, selfish ambition, dissensions, factions** and **envy; drunkenness, orgies,** and the like. I* *warn you, as I did before, that those who live like this will not inherit the kingdom of God.*

Ephesians 4:26-32, 5:3-6

Be angry but do not sin. Do not let the sun go down on your **bitterness** *and thus leave room for the devil...No* **foul language** *should come from your mouth...All bitterness,* **fury,** **anger, shouting,** *and* **reveling** *must be removed from you, along with* **malice.** *And be kind one to another, compassionate, forgiving one another as God has forgiven you in Christ...But among you there must not be even a hint of* **sexual immorality,** *or of any kind of* **impurity,** *or of* **greed,** *because these are improper for God's holy people. Nor should there be* **obscenity, foolish talk** *or* **coarse joking,** *which are out of place, but rather thanksgiving. For of this you can be sure: No sexually immoral, impure or greedy person—such a person is an idolater—has any inheritance in the kingdom of Christ and of God. Let no one deceive you with empty words, for because of such things God's wrath comes on those who are* **disobedient.** *Therefore do not be partners with them.*

Revelation 22:12-16

Look, I am coming soon! My reward is with me, and I will give to each person according to what they have done. I am the Alpha and the Omega, the First and the Last, the Beginning and the End. "Blessed are those who wash their robes, that they may have the right to the tree of life and may go through the gates into the city. Outside are the dogs, those who **practice magic arts,** *the* **sexually immoral,** the **murderers**, the **idolaters** and everyone who loves and *practices falsehood. "I, Jesus, have sent my angel to give you this testimony for the churches. I am the Root and the Offspring of David, and the bright Morning Star.*

Matthew 25:41-46

*Then he will say to those on his left, 'Depart from me, you who are cursed, into the eternal fire prepared for the devil and his angels. For I was hungry and you gave me nothing to eat, I was thirsty and you gave me nothing to drink, I was a stranger and you did not invite me in, I needed clothes and you did not clothe me, I was sick and in prison and you did not look after me.' "They also will answer, 'Lord, when did we see you hungry or thirsty or a stranger or needing clothes or sick or in prison, and did not help you?' "He will reply, 'Truly I tell you, **whatever you did not do for one of the least of these, you did not do for me**.' "Then they will go away to eternal punishment, but the righteous to eternal life.*

James 4:17:

*So for the one who knows the right thing to do and **does not do it**, it is a sin.*

Men. These are somber words. We should not play with sin. It is dangerous and can contaminate us to the point to where we are unfit for heaven. This is why the prayer of the Psalmist is a great one to pray each day:

*Let the **WORDS** of my mouth and the **MEDITATIONS** of my heart be acceptable in your sight, oh LORD my **STRENGTH** and my **REDEEMER**.*

Psalm 19:14

Or another prayer to pray is one by King David after his sin with Bathsheba:

Create within me a PURE HEART oh God, and renew a right spirit within me.

Psalm 51:10

Because of our battle with impurity, getting dirty because of the various sins we commit, we must also pray often *The Jesus Prayer:*

Lord Jesus Christ, Son of God, have mercy on me, a sinner.

And when we pray that prayer, he does have mercy on us! We leave forgiven, clean, with the POWER we need to be an IMPACT MAN.

Last, this can all be simplified by obeying the new commandment given by Jesus.

Love one another AS I HAVE LOVED YOU.

How did Jesus love us? He did it sacrificially. We do it when it's convenient. Not him. He gave us everything. He wasn't out to protect himself, to put himself first. He laid it all on the line. And we are called to imitate him, to love as he loved.

Imagine what your family would be like if you truly did that! How would your wife feel, your neighbor, that irritant person at work… everyone. The world would be changed. And we can be part of that change by loving God and others in the power of the Holy Spirit. The Holy Spirit is in you, all that power waiting to be unleashed if you will only rely on him.

Not by human power nor by personal strength, but by MY SPIRIT, says the LORD.

Zechariah 4:6

So let's go out and do it, in the Holy Spirit's power, let's be IMPACT MEN!

Chapter 2

Sexual Impurity

S urveys show that at the average Mass over 50% of the men who attend are hooked on pornography...that's

OVER 50%!

No wonder we are losing the battle. Men are hooked, longing for sexual gratification, believing that the answer to life is a mind blowing sexual experience that fulfills all their fantasies. Todd even expressed problems in this area.

Oh it isn't that our wives don't get involved in the bedroom with us. They do. But we dream of more, getting more...for ourselves.

And that's it. It's all about ourselves. ME!

A me centered life. That's our real MISSION, what we really want. And that's what sin is..."I" centeredness.

sIn

No wonder why our families, our Churches, our workplaces, or world is not changed. Why? WE ARE NOT CHANGED. We have a gaping hole in our hearts.

This is why the first of this book is focused on intimacy with Christ. That's not just what we need, it's what's driving our desire for women. If we do not fill our souls with Jesus, we will then go after something else to fill that void. Often it's the desire for another woman.

It was Solomon, a few thousand years ago, who was the King of Israel. He had it all, gold, glory and girls - the things men run after. He was richer than Bill Gates, had the fame of any great world leader, and women - Solomon had 300 wives and 600 concubines.

Imagine having a different woman every night, or two or three? Satisfying?

Before you begin to drool, look at what Solomon said about all gold, glory and girls - 900 women who were at his call.

> *Emptiness, emptiness, emptiness, it's all empty, like trying to catch your breath in your hand. You blow into it, close your fist, and then open. Nothing!*
>
> See Ecclesiastes 1:2, 14

So too is all the **GOLD, GLORY AND GIRLS** - all vanity, all emptiness.

Yet today men peer at their computer screens drinking in another orgasm, dreaming, wishing that they could experience that. They masturbate, and all their spirituality, all their power to live for Christ goes out the end of their penis.

All for a moment of pleasure. Never satisfied. Wanting more and more and more.

Samson was this kind of a guy that we read about in the Scripture. He was one of the Judges of Israel before they had kings. And he was some kind of a man - would have been a star in the NFL today, strong, cunning, a great warrior.

But he had his achilles' heel, women.

It's impossible to be an IMPACT man, for God to use you, if women are the focus of your life. And Samson found that out. As he was cavorting with Delilah, the Holy Spirit left him, and Samson was captured, his eyes put out, and he died a tragic death. All because of women. Samson had such promise. He could have been one of God's great saints and heroes. But he sold out.

David, the great King of Israel did the same, lusting for Bathsheba. He paid the price for this one night stand with a beautiful woman the rest of his life.

You see, THERE IS NO POWER WITHOUT PURITY.

You may want to be an IMPACT man, but you will never be a GAPman if you are always looking for sexual satisfaction.

I find, when I am on the internet, I am constantly bombarded with "soft" pornography - whether I am on the ESPN site or some other. There is a constant waving of sex before us all the time. That is why we must fill our souls with the presence of Christ. When there is an empty room in our soul, Satan loves to fill it with something else.

This is why the Impact acrostic begins with INTIMACY with God. Without that, you are prey to everything else. You don't stand a chance.

But with God in your life, you can do anything. He wants to come into that special place reserved for him, to fellowship with you and to bring you an abundance to life that you have never experienced before.

Todd was learning how to do this. Time with God was becoming something that marked his daily life and changing everything about him. It was magic…or better yet, it was a miracle!

For additional materials on masturbation,
read the Catechism, # 2352.

Also remember that sexual pleasure is a gift not a right. And this gift comes with directions for the greatest impact.

FOLLOW THE DIRECTIONS.

The Church (which speaks for Jesus Christ) has given them to us.

Read the Catechism to gain insight.

Talk with your Priest.
In ALL these areas CHECK OUT DEPENDABLE RESOURCES THAT ARE AUTHENTICALLY CATHOLIC.

You many want to buy a copy of the book, **Gold, Glory & Girls**, as well as for other men you know. It's a message that Catholic men need, a message that will help them to see that they need another "G" in their lives…**GOD**.

CHAPTER 3

HOW TO DEVELOP
PURITY IN YOUR LIFE

No purity, no power. It's that simple. You will never be an IMPACT man without it.

How, then, can a man in today's world develop the kind of purity and holiness that produces power?

First, there are the Seven Deadly Sins listed in chapter one of this section.

One of the best ways to overcome these deadly sins and find purity is to spend time in the presence of God. This is why in this book the "I" for Impact is first. Time in the presence of God, an intimate walk with him, will be a tremendous aid to living a pure life.

Read and meditate on the Scriptures. Say the Rosary. Go to daily Mass if possible. After all, you are what you eat. Be regular in the Sacrament of Reconciliation.

If you drink in the things of God, you will begin to live a more pure life. If you drink in from all the other sources of the world, you will begin to think like others around you and will experience defeat. Your heart longs for God. You were made to be inhabited by him and to walk with him. Quit filling it with all the gunk in the world. Let God be at home in your soul. And purity will be yours!

Second, in relation to sexual sin, take the steps listed below. You can be freed from sexual impurity if you will faithfully follow these steps.

1. **ACKNOWLEDGE** that you have a problem. Don't deny it or say, "I'm a man and that's just the way it is with men." If you don't admit your problem and continue to make excuses, you will never be a GAPman, a man of great power, an INTENTIONAL man, a man who lives ON PURPOSE.

2. **QUIT MAKING EXCUSES.** Some guys say: "My wife turned me down last night, therefore I have to relieve myself." Or, "It's better to masturbate than to have sex with another woman." Or, "I've been gone a week on this business trip and need some relief." All the excuses! Sexual solitaire is never the answer. Obedience to God ALWAYS makes us feel the best…in the long run.

3. **CONFESS** it to a priest. Tell it all, the pornography, the masturbation, the fantasizing, sexual sins that occur even in marriage as well as any deep desire for sexual satisfaction that is not in line with God's plan.

4. **GIVE IT UP.** STOP IT, totally. Don't spend time considering a sinful opportunity - wishing you could do whatever is the sexual temptation. Make a decision to stop the impurity each day. Know that the pleasure of the moment will mean guilt the rest of the day. So it's one day at a time. "Today, I will not look at pornography. Today I will not masturbate. Today I will not fantasize."

For additional help, you may want to look at **covenanteyes.com**. Download what pornography does to you and your brain. It shows how pornography actually DESTROYS your sex life. And the information you read is based on science, not just the Bible or Church teaching. If you want to have a beautiful sexual experience with your wife, you will flee from pornography. The site, covenanteyes.com has an internet filtering program if you need it. Thank God for this help!

5. That **EVIL SPIRIT** that tempts won't go away easy. He knows this special weakness you have and knows that you are putty in his hands. You have obeyed his wishes for years. And he has seen you make vows to never do it again. He laughs. "You are powerless when I want you to be impure," he says.

REALLY? I thought that God was more powerful than any other person or force. And this power resides in YOU. With God NOTHING IS IMPOSSIBLE!

6. **THANK GOD** for his power to help you. Don't just ask God for the strength to break bad habits. Thank him for the strength. It is there within you. God lives in you to give you

victory. Pray: "Thank you God that TODAY I will have victory because you live in me. I trust now in your presence."

7. **KNOW** that you are never alone. When you look at pornography and masturbate your guardian angel is there watching, saddened by what you are doing. Jesus is also there. And the Scriptures tell us that we are surrounded by a host of witnesses rooting us on. There are millions of saints watching, seeing everything. Nothing is hidden - what happens in the shower, under the covers, in the mind. All is revealed to the millions watching…

EVERYTHING!

So you think you have hidden sins? Impossible! Your wife may not know. Your pastor may not be aware. But you know, God knows, your angel knows, the millions of saints know and are praying that this impurity would be set aside. They want you to trust in the power of God who is in you, this supernatural strength to overcome any impure habit.

8. **TELL** and confide in another male friend or friends of your struggles and ask for prayer. Be accountable to him, or to your IMPACT GROUP (more later on how to form one). Make sure that there is absolute confidence that what is said in the group stays in the group. And guess what? As you share your struggle, you will find that most other men have the same problems with purity. Man up. Share. Pray for each other. And find victory as you put your shields together and beat back the enemy. Be a team. Be GAPmen!

9. **SPEND TIME** in the presence of Jesus. If you have an Adoration Room, go there often and drink in HIS PRESENCE. Go to Mass often. And put into practice spending time with God in the Scriptures, praying the Rosary, reading spiritual, uplifting books. After all, YOU ARE WHAT YOU EAT.

10. **PRACTICE and pray PSALM 19:14**.

Let the words of my mouth and the meditation of my heart be acceptable in your sight, oh LORD my strength and my redeemer.

Notice that the verse talks about STRENGTH. We need that if we are going to be successful in fighting impurity in our lives. We can't fight it alone. We need HIS STRENGTH. And when we fail, we need to know that we have a REDEEMER, one who will forgive us, welcome us back into his loving arms and be our friend.

PART 4

ANCHORED IN THE FAITH

CHAPTER 1

KNOWING WHAT YOU BELIEVE

The sad thing about Catholics is this; they do not know their faith. They have been catechized, and that's about it. Few men read about their faith and know how to express it in any meaningful way.

Todd was in this camp. He was the typical Catholic man who had great ignorance regarding the Holy Scriptures and the teaching of the Church in the Catechism as well as other basic teaching of the Church. Because of this, Todd bought into relativism which is so rampant today - believing that somehow everyone is right. Relativism insures that there is no theological spine, a backbone that is strong and will stand up to the lies that our culture spreads.

What are the basics that Todd and you should know?

1. **Know the Creeds** - Nicene and the Apostles Creed. Go word by word and make sure you understand what you are saying. The Catechism takes the Apostles Creed and does this. It is rich in its insight. Read it. Ponder on it. You won't understand it all. No one does. We are talking about an infinite God. Our finite minds have trouble wrapping our thoughts around him.

It's like taking a cup full of ocean water and thinking you can understand the whole ocean through that one, small cup. Impossible! Yet, it's amazing how many secrets of the ocean can be understood through taking just one cup, looking at it, really looking at it, sipping it, smelling it, tasting it, feeling it go through your fingers, hearing the sounds. You can't rush this. In fact, you should give your life to the study of HIM who is all and in all. And the amazing thing is this, HE WANTS TO KNOW YOU personally, to walk with you and for the two of you to be confidants.

A helpful book is Dr. Paul Young's, *KNOW WHAT YOU BELIEVE, a Dynamic Catechism for Today.* He teaches you a key sentence upon which your faith is centered. It is a memory system that will get you deep into your faith and belief.

2. **Know the Seven Sacraments.** Be able to talk about them and why they exist.

    1) Know about the *Eucharist,* the Catholic view and why it is unique.

    2) Know how to make a good *confession.*

    3) Know why *marriage* is a sacrament and what difference that makes when contrasted to just getting married in a Protestant church or at the courthouse.

    4) Understand what your *baptism* did for you as well as *confirmation.* What good are these sacraments? What practical value do they have?

3. **Know about God**, his make up and why we believe there is a God.

1) What are a few simple proofs that God exists?

2) What are some simple proofs that the Catholic God is the true God?

3) Why do we need God?

A good book that is foundational is: *If There Is A God...Whose God Is God?* You can find it on amazon.com.

4. **Know about Jesus Christ** and why he is the center of our faith

1) Is Jesus Christ God? What proofs do you have?

2) Why was the death of Jesus important?

3) How do you know that Jesus was really resurrected? Any proofs?

4) How is Jesus important to our Catholic faith...now?

5. **Know about the Church** and why the Catholic Church is the one that Jesus established.

1) Define: ONE, HOLY, CATHOLIC, APOSTOLIC CHURCH

2) Why do Protestants need to come back to the true Church?

3) What is the one requirement to become part of the Catholic Church?

6. Know how to become a Christian
    1) Define a Christian

    2) Are Catholics Christians? Why?

    3) Are you a Christian? How did it happen and what will help you to continue to be a Christian?

    4) What is the secret to successful Christian living?

7. **Know the parts of the Mass** and why each part is important.
    1) Dipping the finger and making the sign of the cross as you enter - a renewal of your baptismal promises.

    2) Genuflecting before the presence of Christ in the Tabernacle - bowing to Jesus your Lord and Savior.

    3) Kneeling before the crucified Christ who wants to give you salvation now and forever.

    4) Rising as the Priest and the Holy Scriptures move down the isle, picturing Christ and his word to us, all the focus of the Mass - Jesus, Words from God. It is here that we sing words of joy - Christ has come and he wants to speak to us - to our hearts!

    5) Confessing our sins and finding mercy and forgiveness

6) Hearing the Scripture, the "Word of the Lord."

7) Listening to a homily - God's word through the Priest - a spokesman for God. Because of this we should listen.

8) Affirming our faith in the Creed..."I believe..."

9) Bread and wine transformed into the body, blood, soul and divinity of Christ - a miracle that should awaken our hearts and capture our attention.

10) We receive HIM as our personal Lord and Savior, Christ Jesus the consecrated bread, the sacred HOST whose body we eat and whose blood we drink. He in us and we in him. Unbelievable! This is our only hope. "Lord Jesus Christ, Son of God, have mercy on me, a sinner." And he does! Through this special grace we are transformed and brought into his family, at each Mass, each time the consecrated bread, that sacred HOST touches our tongue, a miracle occurs...in US. HE is the food that we must have to continue to live so our souls do not get parched, dried up and die. This is why going to Mass is required, obligatory. We need it to breathe, to walk, to have strength, to have HIM, to have life.

11) The Priest, representing Jesus, leaves as we sing a song of hope. It is now our duty, our privilege to take this message of salvation and hope to the world to which we live. We are to go and bring Jesus into our families, our places of work, our neighborhoods and spread the good news.

8. **Know the basics of the Bible** and its message.

1) The first two chapters of the Bible in Genesis start with creation. The last two chapters of the Bible in Revelation end with re-creation. Why re-creation? The answer is Genesis 3, the Fall of humankind into sin. Adam and Eve walked away from fellowship with God. In Genesis 3 there is a promise of a redeemer that would come, through a WOMAN - the prediction of Mary, our blessed Mother. Beginning with Genesis 4 through Revelation 20, we see this prophecy fulfilled and the human race restored through Jesus Christ the King of Kings and Lord of Lords.

The Bible is a story of horrible failure, time and time again. Humankind without God is a disaster. Yet, the Holy Scripture is also filled with hope. We see the end of the story. God wins. Satan loses. And we who are with God, win! Fellowship is restored. We live forever in a new Eden, where all things will be new - no pain, no heartache, no struggles, just pure joy because of HIM, Jesus the source of all joy and peace.

2) Old Testament - 46 books. New Testament - 27 books.

3) If you can read at 1,000 words a minute you could get up and start reading at 6 AM and be finished between 7 - 8PM. Yet most Christians NEVER read all of God's revelation. What would happen if when you get to heaven and God says: "Did you ever read my book?" What will you say? If you say, "What book?", that won't cut it. If you say: "I was too busy," you know that's not true. How much TV did you watch, play games of golf, etc. If you read just one

chapter a day (usually takes just a few minutes) you will be finished in 3 1/2 years. Then you can say: "I read your book!"

9. **Know the Rosary**.

1) Monday - Saturday *The Joyful Mysteries*

2) Tuesday - Friday *The Sorrowful Mysteries*

3) Wednesday - Sunday *The Glorious Mysteries*

4) Thursday - *The Luminous Mysteries*

10. **Know how to pray**. Use the acronym, **A.C.T.S.**

A - doration. Worship God for WHO he is.

C - onfession. Admit to God when you mess up and fail.

T -hanksgiving. Be thankful. Have a grateful heart. St. Paul said: "In everything give thanks." He did not say "for everything" but "in" everything. We don't thank God for flat tires, a cold, cancer, or tornadoes. But we can thank God "in" these times knowing that these things touch us for our ultimate good.

S - upplication. Here we bring our requests to God. Be specific. And always thank him for what he will do as he listens to these requests and seeks to do what is best.

One of the best study sites for men is crossingthegoal.com. They have many free video and written courses you can take that will expand your faith and help you to be a better Catholic man.

CHAPTER 2

BELIEVING **WHAT YOU KNOW**

I t is easy to know about something, but to believe in it, to trust it, is a different story.

When we go to Mass we say the creed - "I believe..." It's easy to say that we believe yet what does it really mean? What we are saying here is BELIEF TO THE POINT OF COMMITMENT - not just a cognitive assent. We can say that we believe in Jesus, but it's a totally different thing to trust him with your life.

Let me tell you a true story that Todd liked very much.

Harry Blondin was the famous tight rope walker from France in the 19th century. One day, he strung a 1,100-foot span across the Niagara Falls, towering 160 feet above them.

Thousands of people were there to watch this event, to see Harry Blondin walk across the raging waters balancing only on a small, thin wire. One slip would mean certain death.

To the awe of the masses who watched, Harry began his journey across the Falls, each step was carefully taken, each puff of breeze had to be critically assessed and countered by shifting his weight.

It took nerves of steel, but Harry was up to the task. As he approached the other side, the crowds began to cheer. Harry Blondin was doing what seemed so impossible.

But Harry was not finished. After the crowd quieted down, Harry was given a wheelbarrow by his manager. He pointed to the wheelbarrow and asked how many believed he could push the wheelbarrow across the Niagara Falls and make it safely to the other side. The crowd cheered in belief. Yes, the great Harry Blondin could do it – absolutely do it!

So Harry took the wheelbarrow, positioned it on the high wire, and began the journey across, all 1,100 feet of wire swaying in the wind, 160 feet above Niagara Falls. It was impossible. But Harry was doing it. Would he fall? Would the crowd see the end of Harry Blondin and his body thrown into the swirling waters of the Falls?

But, to the cheers of the crowd, Harry made it. He was swarmed as he made his way off the high wire with his wheelbarrow. There were pats on the back, smiles of unbelief that he had made it across.

Yet Harry was not done. Motioning to quiet the crowd, Harry Blondin asked another question. "Do you think I could push this wheelbarrow across the Falls with a person inside the wheelbarrow?

The crowd could not believe what he had just proposed. There was at first a wrestling of unbelief. Harry had made it safely across with the wheelbarrow, why not with a person in the wheelbarrow? And, if he believed he could do it, then he must be able to do it.

So the crowd cheered once again approving the fact that Harry could go across the Falls on the high wire pushing a person in the wheelbarrow. The more they cheered the more they believed he could do it. Harry Blondin could do anything he wanted to do on the high wire. If he said he could, he could. That was it!

Harry Blondin then quieted the crowd. I will push a person in the wheelbarrow to the other side. But I need something. I need a volunteer.

At that the crowd grew very quiet. Who would volunteer? And that day, in spite of the great talent and skill of Harry Blondin, no one volunteered. All that cheering, but no one to put his life on the line. So Harry took his manager across Niagara Falls in the wheelbarrow successfully to the wild cheers of the crowd.

Now I have a question for you. Did the crowd believe that Harry Blondin could do it? Yes, in once sense they did. Yet none was willing to stake their life on it.

This story illustrates for us what it means to have true, saving faith or belief. Jesus is quoted by Mark: "He who believes...will be saved."

What does it mean to believe? The crowd believed that Harry could do it – but they would not trust their lives that he could do it for them. They could not move from intellectual assent to personal trust.

This illustrates so many men today, even men who are Catholic. They believe the facts about God and Jesus Christ, after all don't we all say the creed at each Mass? Yet this assent to the facts are not what really brings about a conversion that saves us now and in the world to come. Saving belief is when we put our lives on the line for what the Church teaches. It means that we crawl into the wheelbarrow and allow Jesus to take us through the tough and troubling times in our lives. It means that we will have confidence that he will come through for us. He won't let us slip and fall into the raging problems that are always around us.

Let me ask you a question: What kind of Catholic faith do you have? Are you just believing in some facts or are you trusting in a person, in Jesus Christ who will save you from destruction and give you life now and life for all eternity?

Today we need more men with the courage to crawl into the wheelbarrow, to trust Christ completely with all they have, their family, their money, their jobs, their health…everything.

What are you going to do? Will you stand with the crowd and cheer, or will you get up and do the manly thing, get into the wheelbarrow, trusting your all to Christ Jesus?

CHAPTER 3

PRACTICING WHAT YOU KNOW

S t. James said in his book that "faith without works is dead." A live faith produces a behavior that is in line with what we believe.

Here are some practices that should be part of your daily life.

1. Going regularly to Mass so that you can receive Jesus Christ personally as your Lord and Savior. This is manna for your soul, power to be an IMPACT Man.

2. Confession of sin each day as well as practicing the Sacrament of Reconciliation regularly

3. Praying though the Scripture

4. Praying the Rosary for your family

5. Loving your wife as Christ loved the Church

6. Leading your children spiritually

7. Impacting your Church, workplace, neighborhood, other men

8. Finding POWER in a pure life

9. Walking in obedience to all of God's revelation through the Scriptures and all that the Church teaches.

PART 5

COMMITTED TO OTHER MEN

CHAPTER 1

THE NEED TO BE IN A GROUP
OF COMMITTED MEN

The Bible says that:

> *Two people are better off than one*, *for they can help each other succeed. If one person falls, the other can reach out and help. But someone who falls alone is in real trouble. A person standing alone can be attacked and defeated, but two can stand back-to-back and conquer. Three are even better, for a triple-braided cord is not easily broken.*

> Ecclesiastes 4:9-12

When we read the New Testament we always see the faithful moving in teams not as single individuals. St. Paul almost always traveled in a group or in tandem with someone else. Solo Christianity is not the normal kind at all. We need each other if we are going to have an impact on our families, workplaces and our world.

What does this mean? You need to have a group of men around you who will help hold your feet to the fire as you do the same for them. You will pray for each other, stand up for each other, root for each other, and help each other to be IMPACT men.

So you need to form an IMPACT group.

Todd grasped the vision of doing this, and did it ever make a difference. He followed the steps given in the next chapters. The result? a REVOLUTION!

CHAPTER 2

HOW TO FORM AN IMPACT GROUP AND WHAT TO DO

1. **PRAY** about who you would like to invite to be part of your group. You need *men who are Catholic* or at least willing to look at the Catholic Church and are willing to meet once a week. The need to be men who will be men of INTENTION, men who have a MISSION, who will learn how to live on PURPOSE. God will whisper some names into your spiritual ears as you pray about this. **This is not an interdenominational study and ministry.** Though there are other great Christians who are Baptist, Methodist, Presbyterians, and on and on, they will not be comfortable in our mission - to produce committed Catholic men who will IMPACT their families, workplaces, society and Church.

2. **CHALLENGE** the men you invite to read this book. The IMPACT GROUP is not a place where you come and chat about sports, politics, etc. You are men of INTENTION who have a focus. Your goal is to carry out your MISSION. So you know

what it is (see chapter on mission). Of course you will talk about other things at times. But this is not your focus.

3. **GATHER** together once a week. The commitment is to be in league with each other, to be an encouragement to each other as you carry out your mission. Remember it was St. Paul who said to the leaders of the Ephesian Church:

> *My life is nothing. The mission given to me from Christ Jesus is EVERYTHING. I am committed to the task of impacting my world for Christ. Period.*
>
> Acts 20:24

If, as a group, you do not focus on this mission and just shoot the breeze, you will never make your mark for Christ.

> *Only one life will soon be past*
> *Only what's done for Christ will last!*

SHARE ONLY ON AREAS THAT HAVE TO DO WITH
I.M.P.A.C.T.

If something comes up about politics, it should be talked about only if you are covering IMPACT. How does this discussion of politics help me to walk more closely with Christ, to live more purposefully, or to impact men for Christ? If all we do is share gossip about another politician without sharing a PLAN to bring about IMPACT we are only shooting the breeze and accomplishing nothing. This also goes for sports, women, or any other topic. We gather to be IMPACT men and to help each other to accomplish that.

Period.

Also, pray for each man in your group each day that they truly would be an IMPACT man. And watch as your prayers are answered!

4. Follow **I.M.P.A.C.T.** as you share. Make sure you share and not just report. This time together is not a reporting session, but one where you share your hearts. You are there as a team bent on impacting your world. Some groups take only one letter of IMPACT and focus on that through their entire session (say on I). Others leave it open to what letter or letters men would like to comment on and share.

Open by praying THE OUR FATHER as well as St. Joseph Pray for us. Then share:

I - **Intimacy with Christ.** How was your time with him? What did he say to you this week? What did you learn as you read the Scriptures? Did you journal? Did you struggle with this priority or rush it? Remember what Jesus said: "Without me you can do nothing." We need him in our lives.

M - **Mission.** You discuss what you are doing INTENTIONAL-LY, with yourself, your family, your workplace, your Church, your world. Spell it out. And as a team, you should be looking for young men you can challenge to go into the Priesthood and women into religious life.

P - Power through purity. How are you doing? Where are you struggling? Remember. All things shared in this group are confidential. Be open. Be real. There is power in helping each other. And realize that NONE OF US ARE PERFECT. We all have our struggles. This is why we need each other, to hold each other up, to give each other strength and encouragement on our journey as we seek to IMPACT each other.

A - Anchored in the Faith. What am I doing to know my faith better? What am I reading so that I am INTENTIONALLY deepening my faith and knowledge in what I believe? Do I know my faith well enough to defend it from attack?

C - Committed to other men. One of the goals is to bring another man into the group every 3 months. Discuss who you are praying about asking to be part of your IMPACT Group. To neglect this part is to pass up on the mission of conquering your part of your world. Men must reach men and instill in them the passion for living for Christ, being spiritual leaders in their homes and impacting their world.

T - Triumphant! We need to see that we are on the winning side. When we walk with Jesus and do what he asks us to do, WE WILL WIN! But there are times we don't feel like winners. Share your triumphs, where you are discouraged, and pray for each other. But know the statement St. Paul said to the Romans is true,

If God be for us
Who can be against us!
We are MORE THAN CONQUERORS
Through him who loved us.

Romans 8

To finish, pray the Hail Mary.

Then read your commitment together and make the sign of the Cross.

Now is the time
Today is the day
To begin
And keep on beginning
Every single day
To keep going
To make *MY MARK*
***FOR* Christ and**
***WITH* Christ**
For my family
For His Church
For my community
Forever…Amen

5. You may sometimes close your time praying for those who have a special need, a short prayer like: "God help Mike to be a better father this week. Give him wisdom as he faces these difficult situation with his son." Or, "Be with Fred as he struggles with job issues. Give him peace.".

See further details about the IMPACT groups in the appendix.

CHAPTER 3

THE POWER OF
MULTIPLICATION

...the people who are crazy enough to think they can change the world, are the ones who do.

Apple Inc.

It's amazing what can happen when you live life INTEN-TIONALLY.

The goal of the IMPACT Group is to double every 3 months - each man bringing another man into the group. This is going to take some INTENTIONAL work and planning...and lots of praying.

Who should I invite? Any man willing to make the commitment to be an IMPACT man. Men are waiting for a challenge. They want to live their lives ON PURPOSE but do not know how to do it. The IMPACT Group will help them. It will change their lives and the lives of those around them.

This is why it is imperative that you focus on bringing in other men into the group. Every 3 months the group should double. The only way this will ever happen is each man's commitment to have an impact, not just on their families and places of work, BUT ON OTHER MEN. If we can reach men, we will change our society and culture. And, with Christ, WE CAN DO IT!

This means that the group will have four men at the end of 3 months if you start with two. Then at the end of 6 months you will have eight men. DIVIDE THE GROUP AT THIS TIME no matter what a great time you are having. One of the goals is to impact as many men as you can. If you stay in your nice little fellowship group, you will be the same size in a year, five years, even ten years. In fact, the groups that don't grow will soon diminish in size, meaning that little impact will occur.

When your group grows from 2 to 4 to 8, divide the group but keep a link to each other. There will be natural leaders, and they should keep in touch and encourage each other. Soon from your one group will be two groups, then four groups then eight groups and on and on. Keep a diagram of how your group grows and the leaders of each group.

It can look something like this:

Group 1 (your original group)
Group 2 and Group 3 (come from your original group)
Group 4, Group 5, Group 6, Group 7 (come from group 2 and 3)
Group 8 - Group 9 come from group 4
Group 10 - Group 11 come from group 5
Group 12 - Group 13 come from group 6
Group 14 - Group 15 come from group 7, and on and on.

In time there will be dozens of groups growing from Group 1. It will be fantastic to see many men become IMPACT men.

As your groups grow and divide, you may want to get all the groups together once a quarter for breakfast and once a year for a conference.

You could even begin this in your Church, you and another man, then four men, eight men, sixteen men, and at the end of the year thirty-two men.

Look at what will happen if ONE MAN makes this commitment. It's staggering! When ONE man decides to be a GAPman. The world will be changed!

1. **One man** finding another man and each find another one in 3 months - 4 men
2. Next 3 months - 8 men
3. Next 3 months - 16 men

4. **Next 3 months - 32 men - *One year***
5. Next 3 months - 64 men
6. Next 3 months - 128 men
7. Next 3 months - 256 men

8. **Next 3 months - 512 men - *Two years***
9. Next 3 months - 1,024 men
10. Next 3 months - 2,048 men
11. Next 3 months - 4,096 men

*12.*Next 3 months - 8,192 men - *Three years*

13.Next 3 months - 16,384 men

14.Next 3 months - 32,768 men

15.Next 3 months - 65,536 men

*16.*Next 3 months - 131,072 men - *Four years*

17.Next 3 months - 262,144 men

18.Next 3 months - 524,288 men

19.Next 3 months - 1,048,576 men

*20.*Next 3 months - 2,097,152 men - *Five years*

21.Next 3 months - 4,194,304 men

22.Next 3 months - 8,388,608 men

23.Next 3 months - 16, 777,216 men

*24.*Next 3 months - 33,554,432 men - *Six years*

25.Next 3 months - 67,108,864 men

26.Next 3 months - 134,217,728 men

27.Next 3 months - 268,435,456 men

*28.*Next 3 months - 536,870,912 men - *Seven years*

29.Next 3 months - 1, 073,741,824 men -
OVER ONE BILLION MEN!

30.Next 3 months - 2, 147,483,648 men

*31.*Next 3 months - 4,294,967,296 men - CONQUERED THE
WORLD FOR CHRIST! - *less than Eight years*

All beginning with just ONE MAN - A **GAP***man* who has a MIS-SION, living INTENTIONALLY, on PURPOSE, having IMPACT on this family, workplace, Church, other men and the world.

I know what you are thinking. When I shared this with Todd he said:

"THIS IS IMPOSSIBLE!"

"Yes it is," I said, "without Christ. But with Christ ALL THINGS ARE POSSIBLE!"

"Let me ask you a question," I said to Todd. "Is it unreasonable to impact one man every 3 months? Is that unthinkable - to bring a man into your group, to build into them and move them to impact another man? NO! The problem is this:

MOST CATHOLIC MEN WILL NEVER IMPACT ANOTHER MAN...
IN THEIR LIFETIME!

"That's the problem."

"You see, if you put the real numbers to it, all you have invited into your IMPACT Group in 7 years and 3 months are 29 men. That's it."

"Just 29 men!"

"And if those 29 men reach their 29 men and on and on…you have the BILLION."

"Amazing!"

"The real problem is not the BILLION men, but with you and me."

I then asked Todd: "How many men have you impacted? Have you impacted one, just one?"

"Let's say you reach your 29 men in just over 7 years. Not all you bring in will do that simple thing - impact 29 men. Some, even many will lose interest, lose their focus and not be INTENTION-AL men so that in seven years you don't reach your BILLION men. Are you a gigantic failure?"

"Of course not!"

"Let's say that you only reach 1% of the Billion Men - that's only a measly 10 million men. Would you settle for that?"

"You would do it in a heartbeat!"

"OK, let's say that your groups do not have the impact you hoped, and you only impact 1/10th of 1% of what you desired after 7 years. How disappointing! You now only reach one million!"

"Do you see what I'm saying? Let's project that much of your network breaks down. You reach only 1/100th of 1% of what you hoped. You must settle for only one thousand men."

"That's only ONE THOUSAND MEN, men who will impact their families, the places where they work, their Churches, their neighborhoods, their world."

"FANTASTIC! YOU ARE A MASSIVE FAILURE! YOU ONLY REACH ONE THOUSAND MEN!"

"You see my sarcasm don't you? How absurd…a failure by reaching one thousand men. Wouldn't you like to be that kind of failure!"

"Again, most Catholic men impact zero men."

"ZERO!"

"Of course your goal is still that BILLION. But, if things don't quite work out - when you die you will still have great IMPACT… for the glory of God."

Todd got the point, and I'm sure you are getting the point too. If you only LIVE YOUR LIFE INTENTIONALLY you can certainly reach and impact 1,000 other men in 7 years, EASY…only if you will stick with your mission.

Or, if everything does not work out according to this plan and you impact only one man a year. At the end of 28 years - WHAT AN IMPACT YOU WOULD HAVE! Thousands of men would be marching forward, fully committed to their mission in the Kingdom of God.

Now I'm not the person who came up with this plan to reach the world...Jesus did. He said:

> *Go reach every nation, every person in the world, making sure they are baptized and taught the entirety of the Christian faith.*
>
> Matthew 28

How many was he talking about? THE WORLD - that's billions!

Todd was getting the point when I shared this with him for the first time. And by the time he died years later he had an IMPACT on thousands of men.

St. Paul, one of the greatest IMPACT men of all time said this to Timothy, a man he pulled into his IMPACT Group.

> *The things I taught you, teach others who will then be able to teach others.*
>
> II Timothy 2:2

Look at St. Paul's method.
1. Find a man and help him to become an IMPACT man.
2. Help that man to find another man who will become an IMPACT man.
3. He finds another, and another and another until the world is reached.

Men.

We were made for IMPACT!

Let's go out and DO IT!

A Special Message To Priests and Bishops

****

As a former pastor in charge of a number of pastors under my care, I know a lot about ministering in the church, getting caught up in a busyness that does not pay off in the long run. It took me a few years before I saw the biblical plan, the plan of Jesus and St. Paul to grow the Church, spending quality time with men, discipling them, molding them to have impact within their sphere of influence. So what I have to say I say humbly, hoping that God will give you "ears to hear."

If you are a Priest or Bishop that is reading this section, you can have the same impact that I am talking about in this book. Too many Priests and Bishops get caught up administrating their work and not having the kind of impact they could have if they spent time developing men. After all, you follow in the wake of Jesus. Did he have a lot to do? Of course. Yet he was out to IMPACT the world. How was he going to do that? He knew the SECRET. He did it by spending time with the twelve, developing IMPACT men.

This is your secret too. Get out of the office and into the field with other men. Be a MODEL by showing other men what to do and how to do it. In seven short years you could change your parish, your diocese, your world! And this is not blowing a bunch of smoke. This method works. I have personally seen churches recharged, grow, and have great impact on their communities. It is the Jesus method and is also based on the TIMOTHY PRINCIPLE found in II Timothy 2:2. It is the method that planted Christianity in a pagan and hostile world.

In the next 20 years, instead of the Catholic Church being half the size it is today (and right now all projections predict that) it could be twice the size and more!

I hear from some leaders that: "they are not into numbers."

Really? You don't want to reach your parish and EVERYONE in it, or your diocese and see tens of thousands repent and begin the journey toward heaven?

When the Church started at Pentecost, the book of Acts didn't say that a number of people became Christians. No. It says: "3,000." Later, in a couple of chapters it says; "5,000 came to faith." Wouldn't it be a grand thing to report in your diocesan paper that there were 10,000 baptized in a years time!

Is this only dreaming? Absolutely not. The cry of Jesus just before he left was: "Go to your world. Disciple EVERYONE by baptizing them and teaching them to do everything I commanded you."

And this is not a message just to tell your flocks. It should be the message on YOUR heart everyday as you rise. "What can I do...
TO GO,
TO BAPTIZE,
TO TEACH,
TO REACH PEOPLE for the Kingdom of God?
WHO can I TRAIN to accomplish this task...
TODAY?"

****

The IMPACT Groups are…

Not a program.

Only a movement.

Programs start big and get small. Movements start small and get big. And that's what we want - to impact massive amounts of men who will turn the tide and bring the world back to a God who loves them and wants the best for them.

This is not the kind of national organization that is seeking to get their hands into your pocket. YOU ARE IN CHARGE. If you succeed it is your success. Fail. It's yours. But you cannot fail if you will have a MISSION to IMPACT men, beginning today.

There is no one who will tell you what to do except the Lord. He is your Captain. Listen to him (of course you will always be under the authority of your Priest and Bishop). Do what the LORD tells you to do, and reach the world!

Reach men…CHANGE THE WORLD!

Let's get out and do it…with Christ who started with just a few men. Now look how many there are today!

God said to Ezekiel the prophet, "I'm looking for a man to stand in the gap…a GAPman, but found none."

God said to Isaiah the prophet, " Who will go for me?"

Isaiah's answer was bold and determined, the kind of answer we should give:

HERE AM I. SEND ME!

Let's be like Isaiah.

Let's go do it.

Let's be GAPmen.

Let us go and IMPACT our world!

Chapter 4

A NEW MOTIVATION TO REACH YOUR 29 MEN
and help them reach theirs and on and on

I talk about each IMPACT MAN reaching another man every 3 months (or bringing to the group 4 men a year). This sounds nice to a lot of men, but too many will not have the motivation to carry it out. Procrastination will set in. And after three months, the groups will be the same size because, after all, "we have a great time," and "I don't really see the need in increasing the size of the group and reaching other men."

Realize, though, that we are not just increasing the size of the group but helping to save souls. And a soul is the MOST VALU-ABLE thing on earth. If we save souls, we are going to find great wealth in heaven.

Jesus said to a man who had great wealth: (See Luke 12)

You had great earthly treasure but were not rich in what matters to God.

He went on to say: (found in other parts of the gospel)

Seek first the kingdom of God and HIS right way and all this other stuff will be added to you.

Lay up for yourselves treasure IN HEAVEN where nothing can take it from you.

He who loses his life for MY SAKE will find it.

What value is it if a man GAINS THE WHOLE WORLD and lose his own soul.

So let's say that God tells you that for every soul you bring into the group he will give you the value of that soul, the net worth of the world - **241 trillion dollars** in your heavenly bank account. (the present net worth of the world according to *Global Wealth Report, Credit Suisse, October 2013.*). Would that motivate you? (Of course the worth of a soul is far beyond the net worth of the world).

That means in one year, after bringing four men into the group, you would have 964 trillion dollars. But wait. When one of the men you bring to the group brings another, you get another 241 trillion dollars in your heavenly bank account. And if he brings another soul, you get another pay day.

You can see that over the years you would be worth a lot - trillions and trillions.

Bill Gates or Warren Buffet would not hold a candle to you. You would be one of the richest men on earth.

Now this isn't blowing smoke. When we do the work of God, when we save a soul and they save a soul and on and on and on, you are doing **THE MOST VALUABLE THING YOU COULD EVER DO.**

Do you invest?

How are your investments in heaven? Reach men who will reach men. You will be absolutely and undeniably rich - wealthy beyond measure...

FOREVER!

We're not here to take up space
But by his grace
WE'RE HERE TO TAKE OVER!

PART 6

TRIUMPHANT!

178

CHAPTER 1

DEFEAT IS NOT AN OPTION

Thanks be to God who always leads us in TRIUMPH in Christ.
II Corinthians 2:14

God put us here not to be losers but winners. We have been given a task, a MISSION, to live our lives INTENTION-ALLY, on PURPOSE to IMPACT other men, and in the process to live out what it means to be an IMPACT MAN, in our families, our places of work, our Churches, our world.

The Holy Scriptures speak of our mission in terms of a battle, we are soldiers fighting for the faith. That means that we have an enemy that wants to defeat us. Even as Satan followed Jesus around always seeking to trip him up, so too, the devil is, as St. Peter says in his first book, a lion, going about seeking whom he might destroy.

Satan and all his enemy forces are out to defeat you. And then there is the combined efforts of the world that is set against God. We see it today when there is such a squeeze against our Catholic faith, even our own government is becoming the enemy. Last there is our flesh that is in constant battle - "eat, drink and be merry," as we are tempted to get all the gold, the glory and the girls we can.

With such a force against us, what man could ever stem the tide and be an IMPACT man?

Here's the secret. It takes us back to the first letter of impact - Intimacy with God. He is the answer. Here's a formula"

$$\textbf{Everything - God = Nothing}$$
$$\textbf{Nothing + God = Everything}$$

You see, God is all we need. Who cares about all the forces against us. We have HIM!

To back this up, let me tell you a few stories from the Bible.

In the book of Kings there is this prophet, Elisha, who was being sought by a king and his army. They wanted to do Elisha harm. (see II Kings 6:13-17).

One day, Elisha's servant, Gehazi, went out to get some fresh air. When he stepped outside he noticed that the hillsides around them were teaming with soldiers, men ready to capture and possibly kill both of them.

Frightened? You bet!

So he hurried in and told his master.

Elisha came out and saw what Gehazi saw and then said: "There are more with us than with them."

Gehazi was not stupid. He could count. There were two of them and thousands of soldiers. Had his master gone mad?

Then Elisha prayed: "God open his eyes."

At that, Gehazi's eyes were open and he saw the armies of God surrounding them ready for battle. In an instant he was moved from being a defeatist to one where he KNEW he and his master would be triumphant - not because of their own skills, but because of God.

If you want to see other great stories where the impossible happened, read about David defeating Goliath, Gideon who with an army of 300 overthrew an army of 30,000, or the Maccabean wars where Judas Maccabaeus fought impossible odds. You can read this in I Maccabaeus of your Bible and thrill at the way God intervened.

There was also Caleb, one of the Old Testament greats who, at over 80 years old, asked Joshua that he might be able to conquer the most difficult place in Israel - the hill country filled with giants. And he did it!

No matter what your age, you can be an IMPACT man.

It is true. In the world we live today we don't stand a chance. There are too many on the side against us.

But we have HIM - our champion, Jesus Christ.

WITH HIM we can be an IMPACT man and stand in the gap triumphantly!

CHAPTER 2

VICTORY IS ASSURED

The Bible gives us a game plan for victory. In Genesis 3, we see how through one man, Adam, sin entered the human race. This was the great fall of humanity, and we see from then on human history under the Satanic forces.

But in Genesis 3:15, God gave a game plan for victory - a man born of a woman. We know all about it don't we. For in the Gospels we read about a CHAMPION born in a stable to his mother, that woman promised in Genesis 3:15, Mary, our Blessed Mother. He came onto the scene of history to win back the battle and to defeat the enemy, the devil.

At the cross, the place that looked as if Satan and all the demonic forces defeated the Son of God, Satan's head was smashed and through the Church, Jesus is still placing his foot on the head of Satan under the feet of those who are in his Church (see Romans 16:20) so that we might live as conquerors, victorious, winners.

And in Revelation 19-22, we see our ultimate victory, Satan and his forces are defeated once and for all, and all those who have teamed up with him will perish forever. Those on the winning side will reign with Christ forever and ever.

So today, we go out to conquer. Everyday is a fight. But we have the victory assured if we step up to the plate, accept our role as **GAP**men, IMPACT men who, with Christ, go out to conquer.

I played football at Turlock High School in Turlock, California. In the late 50's, we were undefeated and ranked as one of the best teams in America. You see, in that day, we had a bunch of farm boys who baled hay and were stronger than most of the teams we faced.

It was late in the season that we were playing another undefeated team, Lodi, who used the single wing as their offensive weapon. It was a hard match.

With 20 seconds to go, we were on their 20 yard line, behind 13 to 7. Ron Sarhad, our quarterback, faked a hand off, kept the ball and sprinted to the goal line. The stands were packed with roaring fans. It was 13 to 13 and all eyes were on our extra point kicker who could win the game for us.

The ball was hiked and placed on the ground. The foot of our kicker slammed into the ball with accuracy and power. Within a space of a few seconds we knew…Turlock won. Lodi lost. We were the champs!

So too in life. We could very well be in the last quarter, even the last few minutes of the game. It looks like the enemy is winning. What do we do? Capitulate?

NO!

We are IMPACT men who have a MISSION, who live INTEN-TIONALLY on PURPOSE to impact our world for Jesus Christ. With HIM we are assured of victory.

> *Thanks be to God who gives us the VICTORY through JESUS CHRIST OUR LORD!*
>
> I Corinthians 15:57

St. Paul, who wrote I Corinthians went on to say:

> *Therefore be steadfast, unmovable, always abounding in the work of the Lord.*

That's it! Keep on keeping on.

St. Paul also said at the end of Ephesians 3:

> *Now to him who is **able to do beyond what we would ever imagine or think** according to the power that works in us...*

You can reach a billion men - or at least 1,000 or whatever God puts on your heart. Pray about it. Think about it. Imagine it. Let God put this passion in your heart to be an IMPACT man, and he will do BEYOND what you ever think or imagine.

It's yours - VICTORY.

Amen.

Just an additional note:
In this area of victory and triumph, remember this.

To often we focus on our failures rather than rejoice in our victories.

Let's say you have two failures today but ten victories. Satan wants you to focus on your failures not your successes. Confess you sins, but also confess you victories. Don't be covered over by guilt that will trap you into a life of defeat. Know that you are a sinner. But also know that you are becoming a saint through the power of the Holy Spirit.

Humbly proclaim your victories.

There are hopefully many instances each day where you say "no" to temptation - to lust, pride, envy, greed, gluttony, anger and sloth. Confess these successes. They are yours bought by Christ who promises victory through his Spirit.

CHAPTER 3

86 STICKS OF DYNAMITE

Years ago I was on vacation and one Sunday attended a church in Iowa. In his message the pastor told the story of a woman in the church who needed help clearing her lake of trash fish she didn't want. One of the men in their church said he'd help.

On a Saturday morning, three men from the church showed up at her door with all they needed to get rid of the fish in her lake - 86 sticks of dynamite!

These three got into a row boat, took it out into the lake, prepared the dynamite and then lit the fuse, throwing the dynamite overboard. It would only take them a short time to go back to the shore, get the boat out of the lake and be safe.

But it didn't work out that way.

In the process of leaning over the boat to place the dynamite into the lake, the boat capsized and put the men in the lake where the dynamite, all 86 sticks, were going to explode. And one of the men only had one arm!

You can imagine their panic as they swam toward the shore trying to beat the massive explosion. The man with only one arm beat the rest. Then they sat on the edge of the lake waiting.

Waiting.

Waiting.

When would the dynamite explode? They had lit the fuse, a fuse designed to burn under water.

After waiting 30 minutes they concluded that something had gone wrong. Their mission had been a failure.

> And now
> In a lake in Iowa
> There sits 86 sticks of dynamite
> All that power
> All that potential
> But nothing happened.

And here we are, all that power to become IMPACT men that can and will change our world. It's all there - far more power than 86 sticks of dynamite.

But nothing is happening. Our families, our work places, our Churches, our neighborhoods have not been changed.

Why?

We didn't get it. We never fully embraced our MISSION. We never became INTENTIONAL men, men who live on PURPOSE, to impact our society. The fuse was never properly lit. All that potential.

- All that capacity
- All those possibilities
- Sitting
- Waiting to go off to change our world

But not you.

YOU HAVE DECIDED TO BE AN IMPACT MAN. You are going to make a difference, in your family, your workplace, your Church, your world.

How? What's the plan?

Keep reading.

PART 7

DEVELOPING YOUR PLAN

CHAPTER 1

TAKING THE FIRST STEP

Years ago, one of my sons told me a joke. He said: "There were three frogs sitting on a log and one decided to jump off. How many were left?"

I quickly answered, "Two."

He laughed and said, "There were three left. One DECIDED to jump off, but didn't!"

We both laughed. He had stumped his dad. But I have never forgotten that joke. In fact, as I have worked with men around the world, I have found that there was a lot of truth in that simple joke. So many men DECIDE to jump in and make their mark, to be IMPACT men, GAPmen who will live INTENTIONALLY, on PURPOSE.

But they never jump in.

Decisions. Decisions. Decisions.

That's all.

You know that the longest journey begins by just taking one step. That's it - just one step, jumping in, starting, making that first call to another man.

So it's not just decision time, it's DOING time.

You remember Todd? He did not leave becoming an IMPACT man to chance. He followed this plan and found success. You can too.

The first thing to DO is go through the word I.M.P.A.C.T. and think about each part and what you plan to DO. Get out your calendar and write down dates.

First, you want to begin by starting every day with God in the Scriptures. Set up a journal and begin writing everyday. Pray, meditate, let God talk with you. Report to your Commander in Chief for directions. It doesn't have to be long.

For years I have followed a simple rule - No Bible, no breakfast. For me this works. Find something that works for you. But whatever you do, meet with God each day.

You see, God has his own GPS that will guide you - **G**od's **P**owerful **S**criptures that will guide you each day. That's why the Scriptures and prayer are so important.

Then plan your MISSION with your family. How are you going to be the spiritual leader of your home? You don't have to become mister goody-two-shoes. Be yourself! Yet you can begin to lead in prayer at the meals, pray with your wife, and pray with your children as they go to bed.

You can lay out a plan of instruction - taking short pieces of the Catholic Catechism, or something relevant for your children. Do a Google search and find out what's best. Always make sure it is in line with the teachings of the Church.

Make sure your home looks Catholic - with a cross and possibly a candle that can be lit during family prayer. Our Catholic faith is not just something added on to our lives, but should become part of the fabric of who we are, who the family is.

Most of all PRAY for each member of your family, daily. You can learn how to pray the ROSARY for your family, taking each mystery and applying it to their lives. (See, *HOW TO PRAY THE ROSARY FOR YOUR FAMILY,* by Dr. Paul J. Young. You can find this book on amazon.com.)

Lay out your plans for work, how you can, as a Catholic, penetrate the workplace. You don't have to be preachy. Instead love people - really love them by being kind and generous, optimistic, positive and approachable. And begin to PRAY about whom you might begin a spiritual conversation with, and begin to pull them toward the Catholic faith.

Go through I.M.P.A.C.T. and set goals so that when you plan to jump in you can be this man on a MISSION.

And don't forget the POWER THAT COMES THROUGH PURITY. If you struggle with it, talk with your Priest or another man. You will never be an IMPACT man unless you walk in purity - get all the garbage that is stinking up your life cleared out.

It was Joshua, a great man in the Old Testament, who led the children of Israel into the promised land and showed he was an IMPACT MAN. Not long before he died he challenged the people of Israel to be obedient to God. Here's what he said:

> *Choose you this day whom you will serve.*
> *As for me and my house WE WILL SERVE THE LORD!*

This is your commitment for YOU and for your HOUSEHOLD. Once you jump in, your life will never be the same...to the glory of God!

CHAPTER 2

CALLING TOGETHER
ANOTHER MAN

Y ou remember the goal, don't you, reaching 29 men in just over 7 years and helping those 29 men to reach their 29 who will reach their 29 and on and on until every man in this world is reached and impacted by God.

This is an aggressive plan unlike what you have ever done before. No other movement has a mission like this to impact men. You can be part of something absolutely amazing as you begin to shake your world for Christ.

"But….you say…," and then come the excuses why you can't do this. "I'll just be a better father, a better husband. Isn't that enough?"

Those steps are good, but God has put you here for something far greater than that. He wants you to be the best husband and father you can, yet that's just the beginning. God wants you to help OTHER MEN to be the best they can be too. The kind of mission you feel for your family needs to be shared with other men. They need to be able to live on PURPOSE, to be men of INTENTION, men with a MISSION.

You have learned, I.M.P.A.C.T. and all it stands for. Now is the time to step out and do it. God is there to help. In fact, Jesus has been praying FOR YOU to be that GAPman, to be THE MAN who will start this movement in your Church, in your city, in your diocese.

Of course this means some time each week with a few other men - an hour or hour and a half max. You'll need to meet at a home, a restaurant, at Church, an office, anywhere where you have a degree of privacy, where you can share and pray with each other.

You are going to be building an army, undercover forces who are going to be taking over, men who are going to become generals in God's army, men who are going to be changing their homes, Churches, their places of work and the community where they live.

As men you are not going to lay down any longer and be prey to the society around you. No! God, through you, is going to change this...

ONE MAN AT A TIME.

So, in your journal (you do have one don't you?) ask God to give you some names of men you can invite. Don't invite many at first, just one, two, maybe three. Get with them and see if they are willing to join you in being an IMPACT man. Let them read the book.

You could even buy some books to hand out to men you believe would be open to joining an IMPACT Group.

Take your time. Let the Holy Spirit work. And then, with at least one other man, start your weekly group. Follow the directions of what to do in the "C" part of IMPACT. Read that section and let the Holy Spirit guide you as you become IMPACT men.

Above all, don't give up. You will have a few men drop out. Jesus lost one of his key men - Judas. St. Paul lost some - one was Demas. But keep going. Keep your MISSION clear. Don't stop. And in 7 years you will have one of the biggest smiles on your face as you see men - dozens, scores, hundreds of men who will be IMPACT men because of your courage to take the first step.

CHAPTER 3

WHAT DO YOU WANT?
HOW TO BE A *JOHN 15* MAN

I n the Gospel of John, Jesus asked a couple of men, "What do you want?"

This is ONE OF THE GREATEST QUESTIONS
THAT WAS EVER ASKED.

You remember that King Solomon was told by God that he would give him "whatever he wanted." And, to paraphrase his answer, he asked that he might have a deep relationship with God, that he could hear him with the ears of his heart.

When Jesus asked these two men this question, they gave the GREATEST answer one could give, an answer in line with King Solomon's wish. These men said: "We want to know where you live - where you abide."

Now on the surface this doesn't seem very deep. But these men were not asking for Jesus' address, but instead they were asking for the opportunity to spend time with him - at his place, his residence, his home. They wanted to be AT HOME WITH JESUS.

So Jesus took them, these 2 men, only 2 men to his home. And they started a revolution that changed the world.

Within a day these 2 men reached another 2 men, and on and on. By the time Jesus died there were over 500, then 3,000, then 8,000 then soon there were over 50,000 in Jerusalem who had become followers of Jesus.

How did it happen? Two guys who wanted to spend time with Jesus.

That's all. They wanted to be JOHN 15 men (read this chapter - it's amazing). They wanted to abide with Christ.

You see, you can't spend time with Jesus and nothing else happens. In that quiet time with him you are transformed, made into one of his revolutionaries, a disciple who becomes an IMPACT man.

But IT ALL STARTS WITH TIME WITH JESUS.

That's of course the **"I"** of Impact. You don't start calling other men to be IMPACT men first. NO! You start with Jesus - listening to him in the Gospels, or in the Psalms, or the book of Philippians, or any other book of the Bible, journaling, praying, opening your heart to his desires, confessing your sin, sharing with him your deepest concerns. It is in this time that you become friends that meet each day. And it is from this time together that something happens to you. You are changed and want to impact others.

So…WHAT DO YOU WANT?

If you want to abide with Jesus you WILL BE AN IMPACT MAN. You don't have to try to be one. It will just happen. You cannot spend time with Jesus and have nothing happen. YOU will be changed. And that change will impact your family, your Church, your workplace, your world.

If you think more money, status and women is what you desire - then you may get all this and end your life like so many other men, with a yawn.

But if you want Jesus, then watch out!

The world is waiting for you, and it will never be the same…to the glory of Jesus Christ, the one who calls and equips us to be IM-PACT men.

Now is the time
Today is the day
To begin
And keep on beginning
Every single day
To keep going
To make *MY MARK*
FOR Christ and
WITH Christ
For my family
For His Church
For my community
Forever…Amen

Appendix A

Additional Thoughts On Power Through Purity

In your IMPACT group you may have talked about things that Catholic men rarely talk about - pornography, lust and masturbation. It was open and honest. And I'm sure some may have been shocked by what they heard.

So the question arises: as Catholic men, are we allowed to do this - to be this open with our struggles and sins?

Let me share with you a biblical and Catholic answer.

1. **Sins MUST be confessed to a Priest**. Only he has the authority to forgive that sin.

2. When we talk about our sins or struggles as men with each other, **this is not confession at least in the Sacramental sense.** Yet, the Scriptures encourage us to help each other when we fail, to be the kind of support we should be so that we can overcome our sin and find victory. The Christian life is not a solo life. But too often, for Catholic men, it is. There is never the kind of open sharing that you may have had. Instead, the sin of pornography, lust and masturbation is like the elephant in the

closet. It's there BUT WE NEVER TALK ABOUT IT. And because of that we never get the kind of help we need to overcome these "sins that so easily beset us." (see Hebrews 12:1-2).

3. The Scriptures are clear:

Two are better than one. If one falls, the other will lift up his companion. WOE TO THE SOLITARY MAN! For if he should fall, he has no one to lift him up. Where a lone man may be overcome, two together can resist. A three-ply cord is not easily broken.

Ecclesiastes 4:9-12

I recall reading about the Golden Gate bridge. Each cable is made up of 32,000 strands of wires. Of course, each single wire by itself is nothing. But when banded together, look at the strength! So too with a band of men who are there to HELP each other to succeed in their Christian lives.

Here are a few other verses:

Brothers, even if a person is caught in some transgression, you who are spiritual should correct that one in a gentle spirit, looking to yourself, so that you also may not be tempted. Bear one another's burdens, and so you will fulfill the law of Christ.

Galatians 6:1-2

My brothers, if anyone among you should stray from the truth and someone bring him back, he should know that whoever brings back a sinner from the error of his way will save his soul from death and will cover a multitude of sins.

James 5:19-20

4. So we see the importance of helping each other gain victory over sin in our lives. Of course, the Priest plays a very important part, but we too have a role to play. And too often that role has been neglected.

5. As I wrote before about what to do in an IMPACT group when we talk about our purity and the struggles we have, that **WE SHOULD NEVER BE EXPLICIT** and go into detail about our sin. This is not true confessions! We only share that we need help. We have fallen into the ditch and need someone to help us out. That's it. St. Paul said that: ***there should never be any obscenity or suggestive talk when we share our struggles*** (see Ephesians 5:3-4). Thus we should NEVER elaborate and be descriptive regarding our sin.

For example, a person can share that he is struggling with impure thoughts without going into detail. Or that he is having trouble on the computer with pornography, He SHOULD NOT share what he saw, but only enlist the men for help. In so doing he must also never think that this sharing is somehow a substitute for the Sacrament of Confession (Reconciliation). All he is doing is getting some help to get out of the ditch from some fellow strugglers who may be able to encourage him through lessons they have learned and the successes they have gained. Confession should only be done before a Priest. And every man should be encouraged to practice this Sacrament regularly.

6. In closing, I want to say that what may be happening in your IMPACT group is a learning experience for everyone. Everyone in the group, without question, is committed to grow in their faith and to be the kind of men God desires to their families, at work and in their Church. As you continue the process, you will become a strong IMPACT group and will be able to model how other men can also get together and honestly talk about their lives, pray for each other and thus grow in the process.

Congratulations! You are becoming a band of brothers that can change their world.

Appendix B

Forming and sustaining
IMPACT groups

1. **Gather a group of men.** You can begin with just two Catholic men. There are many other wonderful and committed Christians who are not Catholic, but to bring them into the group will often create confusion about who's right, etc. These groups need to be made up of men who are committed to becoming Catholic IMPACT men. After all, in this group we make the sign of the cross before praying the Our Father - a Catholic act. We also pray the Hail Mary - another activity where other Christians would not feel comfortable. We practice the Sacraments and have a view of the Eucharist that is not shared by other Christians who are not Catholic. So much of what we are and what we practice is foreign to them. This is why we should pray often the prayer of Jesus found in John 17, "I pray that they would be one, Father, as We are one."

If a non-Catholic Christian comes to the group as a learner and is not there to spew his Protestant or other non-Catholic views but to fit into the Catholic mold of the group, that could work. But beware of Protestants or any other person who says they believe in Jesus, who want to join only as a mission to debate Catholic beliefs and practices and seek to "evangelize" Catholics and make them Protestants or get them connected to some other group. They should not be allowed to continue with IMPACT men. Why? It will bring confusion and dilute the purpose for which these groups are gathered.

We are there to share our Catholic beliefs, not debate them. We gather as a band of men to encourage each other in our Catholic beliefs and practices that we might become MORE FULLY CATHOLIC, more fully engaged in our Catholic faith.

When the group grows to the size of 8 or 10, you should divide the group and pick a leader who is responsible for the group and makes sure everyone in the group has a chance to share. He will also make sure that no one dominates. The IMPACT group is for all Catholic men who are committed to making an impact for Christ.

Also make sure that EACH MAN HAS AN *IMPACT MAN* BOOK. One way to do this is to give the person a book when he joins and have him buy a book for the person that he is going to bring into the IMPACT group. This way you pay forward - always gifting the book.

2. You should try to **meet once a week**, before work, at lunchtime, after work, in a home, on Saturday's for breakfast. WEEKLY meetings are the lifeblood of helping you to become an IMPACT man. If you can't commit to this, you will probably go through years spinning your wheels, never accomplishing what God has for you.

3. The IMPACT groups exist for the forming of friendships, the kind that run deep. You are there to help other men and to have them help you in your spiritual journey. **This is not a "bull" session where you talk sports, politics, etc. You are there for one primary purpose - to help you to become an IMPACT man.** Talking about football, etc., can happen after the meeting or at other events. You are encouraged to do other things as men - go to a ball game, play golf, fish, hunt, attend a Nascar event, as well as many other things that men do.

4. There are **five levels of communication**

1) **Facts.** This is the easiest and safest level of communication. You share that you said the Rosary, or you took your wife out for a special occasion, or that you didn't watch pornography that week. These are only facts.

2) **Opinions.** On this level you are taking more risks than just sharing the facts. Others may disagree with you. As men, WE MUST GUARD AT SPENDING TOO MUCH TIME SHARING OPINIONS. This will waste our valuable time and keep us from more valuable forms of communication. So ask yourself: "Is this just an opinion, or is what I am going to say the result of deeper thought?

3) **Concepts.** Here I am not just sharing opinions, but thinking more deeply. This is honest thinking, wrestling with answers (What do I want? How can I get it? What are some possible solutions? Am I doing this the right way?). Opinions come easy. Thinking, true thinking that wrestles with all the options, comes hard. Opinions too often are

not very well thought through. Conceptual thinking takes more time, wrestling, honesty and openness. It is never afraid of the truth.

4) **Feelings.** It is here we share our joys, our fears, our anger, our insecurity, our surprise, our sadness or hurt. This is where we become vulnerable and transparent, taking more risks as we reveal more about ourselves. Many guys feel awkward on this level of communication. It's difficult. We would rather give our OPINIONS than share our FEEL-INGS. But to build the kinds of relationships that bond us together, we must move from just facts and opinions, do some conceptual thinking as well as take the lid off our feelings.

5) **Communion.** Thomas Merton said that the deepest level of communication is communion. He says that this is wordless communication, where words are not spoken. It is beyond speech and concept. It is the bond that we feel as brothers, a bond that is beyond words, a bond that binds us together to be IMPACT men.

5. In your weekly meetings, always start with the "**Our Father**."

6. **As you meet, follow the I.M.P.A.C.T. outline from the book.** SHARE ONLY ON AREAS THAT HAVE TO DO WITH **I. M. P. A. C. T.**. If something comes up about politics, it should be talked about only if you are covering IMPACT. How does this discussion of politics help me to walk more closely with Christ, to live more purposefully, or to impact men for Christ? If all

we do is share gossip about another politician without sharing a PLAN to bring about IMPACT we are only shooting the breeze and accomplishing nothing. This also goes for sports, women, or any other topic. We gather to be IMPACT men and to help each other to accomplish that.

This means that each person will have a chance to share something that happened that   past week. See the card illustrations that can be given to each man in Appendix D.

1) **INTIMACY. What happened when I met personally with God this week?** Here are some things you can cover (but not necessarily all of them):
   - Did I hear God say anything? Though you will probably never hear God in an audible way, he is speaking all the time; words of love, peace, comfort, direction and hope. These words will be thoughts that flash through your mind. When that happens, that is often God speaking
   - Did I write in my journal anything that I can share?
   - Did I read Scripture, say the Rosary, practice another method of communicating with God? What? What were the results? How did I feel?
   - Did I meditate? Contemplate? How did it go? Am I having problems with intimacy with God? Why do you think this is happening? What am I planing to do about it?

2) **What were some things I accomplished in my MISSION** with my family (wife/children), with my work, with my community, with my Church?

- Share if you did anything special with your wife and/or children.
- Elaborate on any problems you are facing. Be real. Talk about your struggles. This is where you can aid others or find help from the group as you seek to carry out your mission.
- ALWAYS remember that this sharing is confidential. Keep it in the group.

3) **Talk about "Power that comes through PURITY."** Share any struggles. Try not to get too elaborate and descriptive. Help each other - don't condemn. This is a struggle that we all have. Face it head on. Pray for each other, and victory will be yours.
   - Were your impatient, angry, or did you spend too much time at work and not enough with the family.
   - Did you love your wife as Christ loved his Church this week?
   - Are you living ON PURPOSE, with a planned mission for your family, or are you neglecting this?
   - What about your words, your thoughts, your meditations?
   - Share about your time on the computer, in a magazine, reading a book.
   - Share about thoughts (again you don't have to go into detail).
   - Share what is helping you succeed to live a pure life.
   - Don't become discouraged with any sin. Success almost always begins with failure.
   - NEVER think that you can't fall. The enemy of our souls is clever.

- Commit to praying for each other that each man would live a life of purity and holiness.

4) **Share what you are doing to ANCHOR yourself in the faith?**
   - What are you reading, listening to?
   - What one thing did you learn about your faith this week
   - Did you learn anything about God?

5) **What are you doing about your COMMITMENT TO OTHER MEN?**
   - Are you praying for each man in your group each day? We are called to shoulder the load, to bear one another's burdens. Pray. Help. Be a friend.Who are you praying for to join the group?
   - Have you passed out any IMPACT MAN books to move men to join the group?
   - Share your problems and successes in this area.
   - Remember, the goal of each man is to reach another man every three to six months. This is the KEY to changing our world. If you neglect this you will never become the kind of IMPACT man you desire.
   - Begin to start praying that God would give you **29 men** who will become part of IMPACT men, men who will reach their 29.
   - What young man are you praying for and encouraging to become a Priest?

6) **In what area were you TRIUMPHANT this week?** Share your successes!

- Success with family.
- Success at work.
- Success in your community.
- Success at Church.
- Success in your personal life.
- Even if you had a ton of failure, you no doubt had some successes. Share these. Thank God for them.
- And remember that all success is ultimately God working in you. Praise HIM!

7) Pray the Hail Mary

8) Close your time together re-stating your commitment:

> **Now is the time**
> **Today is the day**
> **To begin**
> **And keep on beginning**
> **Every single day**
> **To keep going**
> **To make *MY MARK***
> ***FOR* Christ and**
> ***WITH* Christ**
> **For my family**
> **For His Church**
> **For my community**
> **Forever**
> **Amen**

9) **Pray for each other when appropriate,** and then end with a Hail Mary and make the sign of the Cross.

7. **Once a quarter** gather the IMPACT groups together for a Saturday morning breakfast designed to fellowship, share and en-

courage each other to be IMPACT men. At this breakfast you will:

Welcome
Meet three people you don't know
Eat
Interview: Have someone do a controlled sharing where he is interviewed. This lasts 3 minutes. You will cover these questions:

1) How long have you been a Catholic?

2) Was there ever a turning point in your Catholic faith that made it more meaningful? When and how did that happen?

3) How has this change affected your family, work, other areas of your life?

4) What one thing would you encourage these men to do to become IMPACT men?

Talk on one of the IMPACT points lasting no more than 10 - 12 minutes.
Sharing in groups covering questions that flow from the talk for 15 minutes.

Pray silently for the person on your right.

Closing prayer.

This all lasts no more than 1 1/4 hours including breakfast.

8. Once a year you will want to have an **IMPACT Catholic Men's Conference** with focus not just on speakers, but small groups sharing with each other, with men bonding with other IMPACT men.

9. The IMPACT groups also may sponsor sports events, family events, or even bring in a special speaker that would attract Catholic men who are not committed as of yet to be IMPACT men.

10. You can also get involved in the **IMPACT MAN** *University* where you take courses focused on I.M.P.A.C.T. and get your IMPACT MAN degree in three years. There is more on the IMPACT MAN University in the IMPACT MAN Leadership Manuel.

12. There will also be recruiting weekends where you can invite friends as well as other men to learn more about IMPACT MAN. More of this in the Leadership manual.

MOST OF ALL…don't forget to always be looking for men to join your group. It is too easy to become comfortable and not bring in new and fresh blood. If you are going to be an IMPACT MAN you must impact other men.

Period.

Your goal - **29 men**. If you reach 29 men and help them to reach their 29 men you will have impacted 841 men. Wow! You will be rich beyond measure.

Eternity will not be the same.

Appendix C

IMPACT MAN handout cards and other materials

See next pages.

The handout cards can be put on card stock with IMPACT MAN on the front and the commitment on the back. You could even laminate them.

IMPAC✝ MAN

    Begin:Our Father
    Saint Joseph pray for us

Intimacy with Christ
    What did you do?
    What did God say?
    What meant the most to you?

Mission
    Family (wife, children, etc.)
    Work
    Neighborhood
    Church

Power through purity
    Success?
    Struggles?

Anchored in the faith
    What did you learn?
    What are you reading?
    What are you defending?

Committed to other men
    What men are you praying for?
    Who is your target man?
    Problems? Progress?

Triumphant
    Accomplishments?
    Victoires? Praise God!
    Say Hail Mary
    State commitment on back
    Make the sign of the Cross

Now is the time

Today is the day

To begin

And keep on beginning

Every single day

To keep going

To make *MY MARK*

***FOR* Christ and**

***WITH* Christ**

For my family

For His Church

For my community

Amen.

IMPAC✝MAN

We should not neglect meeting together but gather regularly to encourage and rouse each other to love and good works. Hebrews 10:24-25

Begin: **Our Father** and **St. Joseph pray for us**.

INTIMACY with Christ. To KNOW Christ personally, relationally, where prayer is not just a monologue but a dialogue. It is here I move from "churchianity" to true Christianity. *My sheep hear my voice and they follow me* John 10:27. I will seek to meditate and contemplate as I spend time with Jesus.

- What are the marks that my faith is not just an institutional faith but an EXPERIENTIAL FAITH?
- Do I KNOW Jesus or do I just know about him? Give evidence.
- What do I do daily to keep in relationship with Jesus?
- What ways is Jesus communicating with me (Bible, Mass, homily, books, articles I read, prayer, Rosary, Adoration, people, etc.?)
- What problems am I having with intimacy with God?
- What is Jesus saying to me about myself or others? Have I heard him say that he loves me? How did this happen? What else does he say?

MISSION. To live on purpose, intentionally. *I choose to finish the mission God gave me* Acts 20:24. God said to Ezekiel the prophet, *I looked for a man to stand in the gap...but I found none.* God is looking for me to be that man, to stand in the gap for my family, place of work, neighborhood and Church, to be a GAPman, an IMPACT MAN.

- How am I loving my wife and children and helping them to become more like Jesus and grow in the Faith?
- What kind of a witness am I having at work? Who, at work, am I seeking to come to Christ and his Church?
- Who am I praying for in my neighborhood?
- What are my spiritual gifts (teaching, healing, encouragement, etc.)? How am I using them at Church and other places where I can minister?
- What is MY ministry? Describe it (what, where, when, why, how?).

POWER that comes from purity. *Blessed are the pure in heart for they shall see God* Matt. 5. Confession purifies the soul and prepares it for heaven.

- Confess the **Seven Deadly Sins**: PRIDE (I centered), ENVY (coveting), GLUTTONY (over eating, excess), LUST (pornography, adulterous thoughts), ANGER (wrath, rage), SLOTH (laziness, spiritual procrastination), GREED (love of money and things).
- Where am I succeeding, failing, struggling? What is helping me succeed?
- Am I going to regular confession with a Priest? Why? Why not?
- PRAY: *Let the WORDS OF MY MOUTH and the MEDITATIONS OF MY HEART be acceptable in your sight, O LORD, my strength and my redeemer* Psalm 14. How is God giving me strength and redemption?

ANCHORED in the Faith. *Let us strive to know the LORD* Hosea 6.

I cannot know God without knowing something about God. But I can know something about God and not KNOW God. Too many think that they know something but sadly do not know THE SOMEONE - God himself.

- What in the Nicene or Apostles creed do I like the most?
- Do I know the sections of the catechism?? What section do I like best?
- What do I know about God's attributes (love, holiness, truth, power, presence, knowledge, eternal, infinite, mercy, grace, perfection)?
- Do I know how to defend my faith? What needs to be defended today?
- Do I know what I believe but also BELIEVE what I know and put it into practice? I realize that faith is not just faith in facts, but in a person.
- What am I reading, learning, defending?

COMMITTED to other men. *Two people are better than one...three is even better* Ecclesiastes 4. St. Paul was always traveling in a group. I need a band of Catholic brothers who will help me change the world...one man at a time.

- The first step of finding men is PRAYING for men before I invite them.
- Then CHALLENGE them to join an IMPACT MAN group. Give them the book, *Gold, Glory, & Girls.*
- Then gather once a week. This is not only good for them, but for me as we seek to encourage each other to be IMPACT MEN. Weekly encouragement is a must! God has not called me to "solo" Christianity but to encourage others and to be encouraged in my faith walk.
- Who am I praying for (10 most wanted list)?
- What is keeping me from inviting others? What can the other men in the group do to help me? If I invite 29 men in 10 years and help them do the same, this will impact 841 men plus their families! I will make this my goal!
- Who am I praying for that they might become a Priest?

TRIUMPHANT. *Thanks be to God who always leads us in TRIUMPH in Christ* II Corinthians 2. God put me here not be be a loser but a winner. It is so easy to focus on my sins and not where I have triumphed.

- Why is it so easy to focus on my failures than on my successes?
- List success with wife, children, Church, personal life, work, community.
- What other success did I have this week, living out my faith?
- Where did God give me victory? What achievements did I accomplish by God's grace and power?

Say: **Hail Mary**

State commitment:

Now is the time...Today is the day...To begin...And keep on beginning...Every single day...To keep going...To make *MY MARK* for Christ...And *with* Christ...For my family...For His Church...For my community...Forever...Amen

Intimacy: What am I asking God for?

                           What did God say to me?

Mission: Family (wife, children, others)

                           Work

                           Church

                           Community

Purity: Confess (both failures and successes)

                           Offer a prayer of commitment

May the words of my mouth and the meditations of my heart be acceptable in your sight, or LORD my strength and my redeemer.

                                      Psalm 19:14

Anchored: What am I reading that will deepen the understanding of my faith?

Committed to other men: WHO am I seeking to bring into our group?

Triumphant: Where did I succeed?

Appendix D

HOW TO STUDY THE BIBLE IN THE
ORIGINAL LANGUAGES
(Hebrew, Greek)
as an aid for Lectio Divina

Why study the Bible in the original languages? Studying the Bible in the original languages:

1. **Forces you to think more deeply**. You become a detective looking at every detail, the words, the grammar, looking at tenses, voice, and all that goes into making up a language.

2. It opens the door to **discover insights that you would miss** looking just at the English text.

3. It **makes you become more observant** to the details of the text. Because of this you will see much more and as a result apply much more to your life. OBSERVATION is critical to getting good spiritual food from the text. You are forced to look at words and their relationship with other words. You are asking: What? When? Why? Where? How?

4. Your study will **force you to be more accurate** since you are reading the original text of the Bible.

5. Reading the Bible in English is like looking at an 18" television while reading the Bible using the Greek and Hebrew is like watching a 65" LED 1080p HDTV with stereo surround sound! This **gives far more depth and clarity**, all the nuances and richness of the original biblical texts.

The site I use for my Greek and Hebrew studies is **biblehub.com**. This is a free site that is a fantastic aid in going deeper into the biblical text. It will force you to do Lectio Divina.

After bringing up the site, go to the **Interlinear** section (You see this in the section that starts out with Parallel, Sermons, Topics, Strong's Comment, and then Interlinear). You can then type in the Scripture verse or verses you want to study either in the Old Testament or New, or you can bring up an entire section by choosing the entire section. The Old Testament will be the Hebrew text. The Hebrew language reads from right to left, the opposite way you normally read.

On the interlinear site, look at the word in the original language. Above it is a number that you can place your curser on and bring up some great insight into that word. It's invaluable.

There is a commentary also included if you want to follow the text more deeply.

This is a Protestant site so you won't see the 7 books that are part of the Catholic Bible. Be careful when you read the commentary sections. Much of it is good, but you will find some teaching that is not in line with Catholic thought and practice. So beware.

Play around with this site. There are many other Bible study tools that will take you deep into the Scripture and ultimately deep into God. I think you will love it!

Appendix E
Men's Groups and Resources

Thank God for a number of Catholic men's groups and resources that you might be able to draw from to help your IMPACT MAN's group be more productive and effective.

Joseph M. Hanneman in his article in **The Catholic World Report**, May 7, 2015, listed these groups and resources for Catholic Men. They are worth looking at and seeing what may be good for your Catholic Men's ministry and IMPACT MAN's groups and conferences. Though changes have occurred since first printed, I'm sure that there are many that will be of help to you.

Groups

Ancient Order of Hibernians — Friendship, unity and charity for Catholic men of Irish descent.

Catholic Man Night — Meetings and resources to help Catholic men know Jesus.

Fathers of St. Joseph — "A confraternity of men who follow the timeless wisdom and example of the man who was father to the Son."

Fraternus — Faith-building for Catholic men and mentoring for boys.

Holy League — A monthly holy hour with confession and fraternity for Catholic men.

Knights of Columbus — Catholic men's charitable and fraternal organization founded in 1882.

Knights of Divine Mercy — "The quest for holiness and a restoration of the sacred." Monthly adoration of the Blessed Sacrament with confession and fraternity.

Men of St. Joseph — Weekly meetings to instill holiness and facilitate leadership.

The King's Men — Men's groups, retreats, and "Into the Wild" outings.

Wilderness Outreach — An apostolate that "challenges priests, seminarians, and laymen to discover, embrace, and develop their God-given manhood."

Program Content

Ascension Press — Offers a wide range of faith-formation video materials on the *Catechism*, Church history, Bible study, prayer, the Mass, and more.

Augustine Institute — Creators of the acclaimed "Symbolon" adult faith-formation program and the new "Lectio" Scripture study program.

Crossing the Goal Catholic Ministries — Popular EWTN program with a "spiritual workout" featuring Danny Abramowicz, Brian Patrick, Curtis Martin, and Peter Herbeck.

Dynamic Catholic — Matthew Kelly's apostolate offers an expansive set of resources on living a better Catholic life.

Hearts Afire — Small-group faith formation programs and materials from the Marian Fathers of the Immaculate Conception.

Lighthouse Catholic Media — Audio CDs and downloadable talks on a variety of Catholic subjects. Lighthouse has kiosk displays in 5,000 parishes.

Ignatius Press — Offers an impressive catalog of print, audio, and video materials, including the "Footprints of God" documentaries, saint biographical films, and much more.

My Catholic Faith Delivered — Offers online courses from grade school through adult faith formation.

Paradisus Dei (TMIY) — Creators of the "That Man is You!" faith-formation program and the new "Choice Wine" program for married couples.

St. Paul Center for Biblical Theology — A research and education institute founded by Scott Hahn. Resources include weekly "Breaking the Bread" audio commentary on Sunday readings, and a free smart-phone app.

The Mary Foundation (CatholiCity) — Free CDs, booklets, novels, and online resources.

The Reason for Our Hope Foundation — Books, homilies, talks, and more from the dynamic Father Larry Richards, author of *Be a Man!*

Word on Fire Catholic Ministries — Homilies, articles, Scripture reflections, teaching programs, and award-winning documentaries from Father Robert Barron. Includes the *Catholicism* series and the new *Priest, Prophet, King.*

Other resources

Battle Ready Strong — An apostolate from Doug Barry to help "encourage the fighting spirit in all Christians."

Catholic Answers — Premier apologetics organization has a vast library of materials that explain and defend the Catholic faith.

Catholics Come Home — Producer of "evangomercials" seen by 125 million people, and an EWTN television program by the same name.

Catholic Dads Online — A news and information site to help connect Catholic dads.

Catholic Information Service — Downloadable booklets on a range of Catholic subjects, plus an online Catechism and distance education courses. A service of the Knights of Columbus.

Catholic Man Project — Randy Hain's *Journey to Heaven: A Roadmap for Catholic Men.*

Catholic Speakers — Booking service for many popular Catholic speakers.

Chastity Project — Information on chastity, virtue, real-life Catholicism, womanhood, and Theology of the Body.

Defenders of the Catholic Faith — Apologist Steve Ray's well-stocked website includes films, audio presentations, books, and other resources to help Catholics know and defend the faith.

Fathers for Good — Interactive information and resources to help men be better fathers and husbands. Published by the Knights of Columbus.

National Fellowship of Catholic Men — Non-profit organization dedicated to establishing a men's conference in every US diocese.

New Evangelization Ministries — Deacon Ralph Poyo's site to help build stronger Catholic parishes.

Real Men Pray the Rosary — An apostolate that promotes stronger devotion to the Holy Rosary.

Redeemed Online — Weekly videos and other social media content to spread the Gospel message.

St. Joseph's Covenant Keepers — A network of Catholic men helping each other live out their vocations as husbands and fathers.

The Catholic Gentleman — A truly unique "man site" with apologetics, commentary, and the finer points of beer and pipe-smoking.

The Integrated Catholic Life — A vast trove of information on integrating faith, family, and work life.

The Porn Effect — Helping free men and women from addiction to pornography.

Truemanhood — "Teaching virtue while fighting porn and 'cultural manhood.'"

Be sure and buy the companion copy for this book **How To Be An IMPACT MAN, Leader's Guide**. It will help you to be successful as you begin lead your IMPACT Group. You can get it on amazon.com.

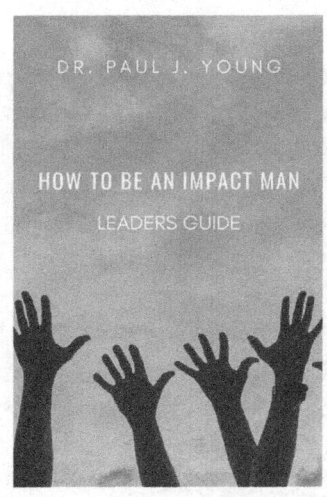

This book will also give further help on IMPACT MAN ministry, see how to conduct an **IMPACT MAN *University*** and **IMPACT MAN Retreat** which will help you to grow and bring more men into the IMPACT MAN movement.

You will also want purchase a copy of **IMPACT MAN** Daily Walk. It has 365 readings designed just for men, with the issues they face each day that will help them to become IMPACT men. It's a book that will change your life! This is a MUST daily reading for you and men in your IMPACT MAN group.

You also encouraged to get the **IMPACT MAN Daily Journal**. This will help you to live INTENTIONALLY, ON PURPOSE each day, becoming the kind of IMPACT MAN God desires.

To introduce the men's ministry, be sure and give every man a copy of **Gold, Glory and Girls**. It speaks directly and EXACTLY to where the average Catholic man is and what he needs to do to find that elusive purpose, peace and joy he is looking for.

Dr. Paul Joseph Young

Who is Dr. Paul Joseph Young?

Dr. Young, a former Evangelical Protestant pastor and leader, has been a Catholic since 1999. While a Protestant, he helped grow one of the largest high school youth programs in the nation, a group numbering 400 wild, exciting and responsive kids.

He then moved to Fort Worth, Texas where he became pastor of a small church of 200. Within nine years it became one of the largest churches in the Dallas Fort Worth area, with thousands coming to worship God. Over 50% of the growth were new converts who came into a living relationship with Jesus Christ.

From there, Dr. Young became CEO of CBS International, an in-depth Bible study movement that grew from a few countries to over 60 countries in the world with thousands of people studying the Holy Scriptures in over 40 languages. It was during this ministry, traveling the world, that Dr. Young became Catholic. You can read his conversion story in the companion guide to the novel he wrote, *Lethal Discord.*

Dr. Young has planted over 90 churches throughout the world, seen over 100,000 conversions, and impacted many men and women to follow Christ. As a Catholic, he helped begin the men's ministry with Emmaus Journey, wrote *Reaching Catholic Men,* and now helps lead the…

IMPAC†MAN, IMPAC†WOMAN movement.

All the things accomplished by Dr. Young have only been through the strength, power and grace of God. Without Christ, Paul could have done nothing…period!

He is married to his wife and great friend, Diane. They have 5 children and 14 grandchildren. Paul and Diane lived in Santa Rosa, California for a number of years, working with their Church and Diocese and have recently moved to Freeland, WA on Whidbey Island, to be close to their son and family.

Dr. Young has been an IMPACT man most of his adult life beginning at age 15 when he started a movement on his high school campus to reach his fellow students. Soon a group of 30 grew to over 120, and a number of his buddies met around the flagpole to pray each morning before classes began.

From that day to today, Paul's drive to impact men and women has not abated.

He wants to help you change and IMPACT your family, neighborhood, place of work, Church and your world.

Let's do it!

Dr. Paul J. Young

Education:

California State University, Fresno, B.A in English

Dallas Theological Seminary, Th.M (Masters in Theology)

Biola University, Doctor of Ministry with emphasis on psychology (working with Talbot School of Theology, Rosemead School of Psychology and other schools)

OTHER BOOKS BY DR. PAUL

1.   Once Divided, a Catholic Thriller. This has been called a "page turner" by many who read it. You will live the story and learn about your faith as you read this compelling novel.

2.   Once Divided companion guide with questions that will help you dig deeper into the novel.

3.   Great Men of the Bible - Saint Paul, his secret to success. The story of his success can be yours!

4.   The Personalized Bible, Philippians. This book will help you to make right choices about feeling great. I take the book of Philippians, a book in the New Testament, and write it as if it were written to YOU. Reading this book for 30 DAYS in a row could have a great impact on the joy you experience every day.

5.   Amazing Women of the Bible - women you never knew before. Read this dramatic presentation of these great women! You will not be the same.

6.   Know What You Believe - the catechism for today. A simple way to learn what you believe, a method for you and your family can use that will give you a depth of understanding of your Catholic Faith.

7. You Can Change Your World - a powerful book that gives us the secret to changing our world. It's explosive!

8. How To Finish Well. A Catholic book for Retired men who want to make the most of their retirement.

9. Potato Salad for the Depressed Soul - Magical steps to take to blast away depression while making potato salad! This is a crazy book that could change your life and bring the joy you are looking for.

10. TOTAL RELIEF SYSTEMS SERIES (3 books in each category - 9 books total). These are books written to help people overcome their emotional struggles and find peace, purpose, and joy. They take a person into an in depth journey to find restoration and healing for their souls.
  • **Dr. Paul's TOTAL RELIEF -** Depression
  • There are *NINE books in this series*, books that will liberate you from depression and anxiety, setting you on the pathway toward JOY, the kind of life you dreamed of.

11. The Encyclopedia of Triggering Events. There are so many things that happen to us with interpretations that guarantee that we feel bad. Want to change your interpretations and actions so you feel a lot better? This is a must read. It will TRAIN you to think and act right.

12. The NOTE. Why has the music left my soul? What is life all about? How can I get music back into my inner being, a song that fills me with hope and joy? This book is both a visual and verbal parable about the NOTE and how he can change you life...NOW!

13. 30 Days To Making Your Wife Feel Special. This book could radically change your marriage...in only 30 days. Take the challenge. You nor your wife will be the same.

14. If There Is A God, Whose God Is God? Who's right, the atheists? The agnostics? What about the eastern religions, or the Jews, or Islam? And then all those Protestants...why do Catholics believe that the Church is really Catholic? Lots of questions. Lots of answers. It will be a faith-building adventure.

15. The Unexpected Visitor. What would happen if you opened your front door and saw Jesus standing there, wanting to come in a stay for a few days. What would you do? How would you act? Would you make any changes? This book delves into a couple who had to allow Jesus to stay with them and the changes it made in their lives.

16. How To Be An IMPACT MAN - a powerful book that will help men to become spiritual forces in their homes, Churches, workplaces and the world.

*This book is also published in a young adult edition designed for college student and young single men.

17. The IMPACT MAN *Daily Walk* - a daily devotional for men that will take them to another level in their walk with God. It's practical and powerful! (also in a Young Adult edition).

18. How To Be An IMPACT WOMAN - a powerful book that will help women to become spiritual forces in their homes, Churches, workplaces and the world.

19. The IMPACT WOMAN *Daily Walk.* This daily read includes all the books of the Bible from Genesis to Revelation with each day focusing on I.M.P.A.C.T. Reading it every day will revolutionize your life.

20. GUARANTEED RECOVERY from a loss. Have you lost something dear, a relative, friend, home, job, reputation or money? This book is for you. I teach a simple T.A.P. technique for overcoming loss and finding peace and joy again.

21. Gold, Glory & Girls. What do men want? What do they really want and need? This book takes them on a journey to the forth "G" that men need…GOD and the fulfillment that brings to their souls.

22. I'm Praying The Rosary For YOU! This is a unique book you can send to your relatives and friends showing how you pray for them. In so doing, it will not only change them…it could change YOU!

Look for coming books at **DrPaulPress.com**

A DRPAULPRESS.COM **publication**

I would appreciate if you would **give me a good review of this book.** A good review (4 or 5 stars) encourages people to read the book and hopefully change their lives. Thank you for taking the time to do this. Go to this book title at <u>amazon.com</u>.

My prayer for you:

May God give you courage

To be an IMPACt man

To reach your 29 men
And impact your
Family
Workplace
Church
World
Today
Tomorrow
Until you die
For the glory of Christ
Amen

Made in United States
Orlando, FL
16 February 2024

43748495R20134